NAHC
Wild Game Cookbook

Edited by

Ron Larsen, Colleen Ferguson

Design and Typesetting by

Kenneth Kaiser

Published by the North American Hunting Club
Minneapolis, MN 55343

We would like to thank the following for their help:

NAHC Members, for sending us the original wild game recipes that are the backbone of this 1994 NAHC Wild Game Cookbook. These recommended recipes from your fellow NAHC Members are true taste treats.

The authors, NAHC's Bill Miller, NAHC Member Don Brown, Louis Bignami, NAHC Member Wayne Martin and humorist Jim Shockey for their wonderfully entertaining articles.

The photographers, Len Clifford/Leonard Rue Enterprises, Judd Cooney, Neal and Mary Jane Mishler, Len Rue Jr. and Leonard Lee Rue III.

NAHC staff members, for their diligence and hard work in seeing that this was accomplished in the professional manner to which NAHC Members have become accustomed: Publisher Mark LaBarbera, Managing Editor, Books Ron Larsen, Associate Editor, Books Colleen Ferguson, Editorial Assistant, Books Victoria Brouillette, Art Director Mark Simpson, Desktop Publishing Specialist Ken Kaiser, Vice President of Product Marketing Mike Vail, Asst. Vice President/Marketing Manager, Books Cal Franklin and Marketing Project Coordinator Jackie Ochsner.

Cover photo by George Barnett.
Illustrations by Ken Kaiser.

*Address reprint requests
and orders for additional cookbooks to:*
NAHC Cookbook Editor,
P.O. Box 3401
Minneapolis, MN 55343

Library of Congress Catalog Card Number 84-649847

ISBN 0-914697-57-9
Copyright 1993, North American Hunting Club

The North American Hunting Club offers a line of hats for hunters. For information, write: NAHC, P.O. Box 3401, Minneapolis, MN 55343

Contents

The Joy Of Hunting

The joy of hunting ... with the challenges and stress that each of us faces every day, it's understandable that we may overlook the basic reason why you and I hunt—for the joy of hunting.

Let's face it, it's fun—pure and simple. That's why we've chosen the joy of hunting as the theme for this year's cookbook.

Of course, we may find hunting fun for different reasons. Perhaps it's the rush of adrenaline when you pit your abilities against that of a game animal in the wild, or because hunting puts you at one with nature, or simply because of the camaraderie that grows within a group of hunters who are all savoring life at its fullest.

Really the reason the NAHC was created 16 years ago was to honor and share the joy of hunting. Back then Paul

Burke, Jr., my father, looked around at all the existing hunting organizations and publications. He saw that none existed specifically for the sportsman whose No. 1, year-round, full-time joy was hunting. To fill that empty niche he created the NAHC. I was fortunate enough to be in a position to work with him in achieving that dream of enhancing fellow outdoorsmen's joy of hunting. The rest, as they say, is history.

Since then, I've been blessed with opportunities to hunt with a number of our members, and each time I've come away with a wonderfully warm feeling. To be among hunters who exhibit such high ethical standards and strong senses of fair play and sportsmanship is truly an honor for me. Their great respect for our natural resources makes me proud to be a hunter.

When the sport of hunting comes under attack from outside interests, it becomes easier for those of us who have a great love of hunting to become defensive about our beloved sport. There is no need to become defensive because that only robs us of our love for the sport.

That's not to say that we should stand idly by while those who have little knowledge and understanding of what hunting is all about try to destroy the sport. We should let our opinions and feelings be heard ... but in a very positive manner. We should arm ourselves with facts and calmly and patiently answer each and every attack that is launched at hunting.

We should go about the business of enjoying our sport, and not be reluctant to tell people why we enjoy the sport the way we do. That really is the purpose of this year's theme for the NAHC cookbook—to spread the word about the joy of hunting and to remind ourselves that it's all right to feel good about the sport.

Spread throughout the book, you'll find stories about the good that hunting has to offer. NAHC Executive Director Bill Miller leads off with his reflections on what the real thrill of hunting is. To him, it is setting strict ethical standards and then meeting them in each and every instance—even if others don't know that those standards have been met. What he is talking about is that little inner voice we all have that keeps us on the right path.

I know everyone will enjoy the exciting big-game hunt

stories. Both are testimonials to the joy and excitement of hunting, and in the case of the ram story you will sit in on a very special event—the bonding of a man and his young son. Also, you will read about the bonding that is created when veteran hunters reach out to encourage the novice hunter or the hunter who doesn't care to go out alone. Finally, there is a humorous-nostalgic story about the very special bonding between life-long hunting buddies. You will also find all those tasty, mouth-watering recipes for a wide array of wild game.

Sportsmanship ... family bonding ... wonderful friendships ... and just plain good fun. Isn't that what hunting is all about? Great hunting!

Steven F. Burke
NAHC President

Cookbook Abbreviations

tsp.	=	teaspoon
T.	=	tablespoon
pt.	=	pint
oz.	=	ounce
pkg.	=	package
qt.	=	quart

Measurement Conversions

1 pinch	=	less than 1/8 tsp.
1 T.	=	3 tsp.
2 T.	=	1 oz.
4 T.	=	$1/4$ cup
5 T. + 1tsp.	=	$2/3$ cup
8 T.	=	$1/2$ cup
10 T. + 2 tsp.	=	$2/3$ cup
12 T.	=	$3/4$ cup
16 T.	=	1 cup

1 cup	=	8 oz.
1 pint	=	16 oz.
1 quart	=	32 oz.
1 gallon	=	128 oz.

1 cup	=	$1/2$ pint
2 cups	=	1 pint
4 cups	=	1 quart
2 pints	=	1 quart
4 pints	=	$1/2$ gallon
8 pints	=	1 gallon
4 quarts	=	1 gallon
8 gallons	=	1 bushel

The Real Hunting Thrill For Me

by Bill Miller
  Executive Director
  North American Hunting Club

Hunting coats laden with carefully counted and categorized shells hung across the banister in the back hallway. Meticulously cleaned and oiled shotguns were cased and waiting in the corner behind the door. In the kennels, three enthusiastic springers whined to get going.

But in the kitchen was a pouting teenager. He was sitting backward on a kitchen chair with his chin resting on top of its vinyl upholstered back. His tear-dampened stare was dour at the day and was fixed out the big bay window. The rain wasn't letting up.

The lad was trying to look between the falling sheets of water, hoping to see the slightest hint that the storm might pass. But to the west loomed nothing but mile after mile of gray sky and falling rain.

The noon opener of the Wisconsin pheasant season was less than five minutes away and at age 13, my second season of being allowed to carry a loaded gun while hunting, I couldn't believe I was sitting at home. My Gosh! ...

this was pheasant season afterall!

In the living room, my dad was calmly stretched out on the La-Z-Boy reading the paper. And, at the moment, he seemed like the most ridiculously stubborn man in the world. I couldn't believe he didn't understand that a little rain, well torrents of rain, wouldn't melt us, the dogs or the guns!

What failed to impress me then, but I now remember with a grin, was that dad's Redwing boots were already laced tightly around his ankles and the lanyard of the dog whistle was already looped around his neck. Though he had to put on the facade of fatherly wisdom which dictated "no man in his right mind would go out in weather like this," inside he wanted to have his nose pressed against the kitchen window, too. After all, this was the pheasant-season opener.

Today, I look back on that soggy pheasant opener as a pleasant memory and also a lesson. And, as my wife can tell you, I show no signs yet of "wisdom." When the chance to hunt comes, I'm going—come high water or not!

That's how much I love hunting.

In fact, to convey my feelings allow me to take some liberties with the often-quoted refrain of a lovesick suitor. You know the one: "Oh hunting, how do I love thee? Let me count the ways. I love thee to the depth and breadth and height my soul can reach ... "

Pretty gooshy stuff, but actually listing the reasons why I love hunting is without question an almost impossible task. Even answering the question "Why do you love hunting?" is like trying to answer another serious question, "Why do you love your mother?" But if you think about it for a moment, the answers to both questions could be: "Because she/it made me who I am."

Well, at least it's the start of a good answer.

Those of us in the hunter's mold only know that we love hunting when we are doing it and when we are dreaming about it—which for most of us is all the time.

If I had to narrow the explanation of my love for hunting down to just one reason, I would have to say it is that hunting represents the most satisfying test of ethics and devotion to personal standards that I've ever experienced.

In every hunting situation, the hunter must decide if he is going to stick to not only the law, but to his own code of personal standards.

Let's face it. In almost every hunting situation, it would be possible to violate society's laws and never be caught. Such is the woefully understaffed and underfunded condition of the federal and state wildlife enforcement divisions. However, it should go without saying that the personal standards of all North American Hunting Club Members include knowing and abiding by the established game and fish regulations. As these rules become increasingly complex, understanding and abiding by all of them cam be an interesting challenge.

But, it's contemplating, establishing and abiding by a personal set of standards—a code of ethics—above and beyond the written regulations that make hunting such a personally satisfying sport. Living by a standard of "just because it's legal doesn't necessarily make it right" is tremendously gratifying for me.

On opening day, for example, a young ruffed grouse flushes in front of my springer spaniel, landing on a tree branch—visible and well within shotgun range. According to my personal code, I only shoot healthy upland birds and waterfowl on the wing. Still, there is temptation in the form of my alter-ego that questions my decision.

"This bird's not too bright," it says. "Chances are he'll end up as fox food anyway. And, it's so early in the season, the dog could stand some retrieving practice. Besides, who's going to know?" When you're showing the guys back at the office a picture of your opening-day limit, they would never know whether you shot all of them out of the trees, off the ground or in the air. But you know.

Flushing those birds again and even missing that tough dropping shot will be a more satisfying feeling than polishing off a dinner of grouse that didn't have a sporting chance.

For me, the true satisfaction from hunting or harvesting game must take place under the ethical terms I have established, not merely on the basis of fate or luck.

How then can I explain the times when I've happily, contentedly passed up a 10-point buck one day to happily, contentedly take a spike buck the next? Why, it's very

easy. At this stage in my hunting career, the situation surrounding the harvesting of an animal outweighs consideration of the animal's size. It's the conditions and self-imposed restrictions under which the hunt was conducted that, to me, make an animal a trophy. It's not just how much bone the critter happened to grow on top of its head. If that were the consideration, I would become a shed collector.

Perhaps the best way to describe why this aspect of personal gratification derived from hunting is so appealing is to quote from a story about hunting with my dad that I, as a teenager in high school, wrote for a composition class. It's titled "In The Sun," and it is the true story about a grouse hunt in northern Wisconsin that almost didn't take place because of the weather.

"Orion, the god of the hunt, smiled on us that day because just as I hoped, the rain did let up shortly after noon. The hunt could begin.

"We hadn't walked more than 200 yards from the car,

when I glanced down an overgrown, barely discernible trail and saw a grouse on the ground, completely unaware of our presence. I brought the gun to my shoulder, but knew I wouldn't shoot. Instead I eased two steps forward and yelled, 'Git bird!'

"In compliance with that request, the bird 'got,' catapulting from the soggy, golden carpet of leaves with an explosive take-off, traditional of the ruffed grouse race.

"As much as by instinct as by skill, I brought the gun to my shoulder, swung ahead of the hastily departing wisp of brown and fired. The bird never knew what hit him.

"Only after I hand-marked and retrieved the bird did I become conscious of the fact that Dad had witnessed this whole show from 20 yards to my left. When I turned to him for approval, holding the bird high, I got it and more.

"This man had just seen his son do something he had been waiting for since the first time he had taken the boy hunting 10 years before, since the first time he had let him carry a gun, since the first time he had introduced the boy to his cronies in deer camp."

Since that hunt so many years ago, I'd have to say my hunting horizons have broadened significantly. I've been blessed with opportunities to hunt from the Arctic to Mexico. I've got my eye on trips to Argentina and Africa someday, too. And I'll keep hunting as much and as long as possible so long as each adventure continues to produce the same warm, good feeling—the reason I love hunting.

Venison
Recipes

Marinated Venison Fillet

Serves: 4
Prep Time: 4 hours

2	lbs. venison backstrap or steaks
1/2	bottle barbecue sauce
1/2	bottle Italian salad dressing
1	tsp. garlic powder
1	tsp. onion powder
12	dashes Tabasco sauce
1/2	tsp. black pepper
1	tsp. A-1 steak sauce
1 1/2	T. olive oil
1	lb. bacon

Slice meat into strips as thick as a bacon slice. If using small backstraps, freeze two together and slice when frozen. Pierce each slice with fork. Combine remaining ingredients, except bacon, to form marinade. Soak steaks in marinade for 4 hours. Wrap each strip with bacon slice and secure with toothpicks. Place wrapped strips on grill. When juices start to run on top side, turn and cook for a few minutes. Do not overcook. Serve with mushrooms and baked potatoes.

Artie Hegstrom
Inkster, North Dakota

Did You Know ...

NAHC Members purchased 5.4 million boxes of factory-loaded ammunition in one year. That amounted to 13 boxes per buying member.

Bob And Helen's Venison Sausage

Serves: yields 5-7 rings; 23-30 links
Prep Time: 1-2 days

5   lbs. venison, coarsely ground
3   lbs. pork butt, finely ground
2   lbs. pork fat, finely ground
3   garlic cloves, pressed
1   pt. ice water
1   T. sugar
2   T. kosher salt
1   T. black pepper
1   tsp. allspice, ground
1   tsp. nutmeg, ground

Press garlic into water and store in refrigerator. Mix all dry ingredients in jar and set aside. In large bowl, thoroughly knead meat. Sprinkle dry ingredients evenly over meat and knead again. Add garlic-water and knead thoroughly again. Stuff sausage casings immediately. Tie ends of casings with twine. Hang on rod at 25-35 degrees for 1 day, 12 hours. Then, gently simmer for 7 minutes. Remove meat from pot and slice into bite-sized pieces. Finish cooking in hot frying pan with oil until lightly browned.

Bob Frederick
New Britain, Connecticut

Did You Know ...

Some 272,000 NAHC Members are bowhunters. That's 54 percent of the club's total membership (there are more than 500,000 NAHC Members).

17

Venison Meatballs

Serves: 4
Prep Time: 45 minutes

1 lb. ground venison
2 T. Worcestershire sauce
1 tsp. sage
1 tsp. cumin
1 tsp. oregano
1 tsp. salt
1 tsp. onion or garlic powder

Combine all ingredients, mixing thoroughly by hand. Roll into 1-inch balls and arrange on cookie sheet. Bake at 325 degrees until brown, about 20-25 minutes. Pour off excess liquid and brush with your favorite barbecue sauce.

Noel Garrett
Gambrills, Maryland

Mike's Venison Meatballs

Serves: 4-6
Prep Time: 45 minutes

1 lb. ground venison
1 egg
1 cup Rice Krispies
1 tsp. salt
1/4 tsp. pepper1

1 T. onion, chopped
3 T. brown sugar
1/4 cup catsup
1/8 tsp. nutmeg
    tsp. dry mustard

Combine venison, egg, Rice Krispies, salt, pepper and onion; mix well. In separate bowl, combine brown sugar, catsup, nutmeg and mustard. Add one-half of this sauce to venison mixture, blending thoroughly. Shape mixture into ping-pong-sized balls and place in casserole. Cover with remaining sauce. Bake at 400 degrees for 30 minutes.

Mike Neilson
Danville, Indiana

Sweet And Sour Meatballs

Serves: 4-6
Prep Time: 1 hour

- 1 lb. ground venison
- 4 cups bread crumbs
- 1 egg
- 1 small onion, chopped
- 1 large garlic clove, minced
  cooking oil
- 1 can golden mushroom soup
- 2 T. vinegar
- 1 can stewed tomatoes
- 2 T. brown sugar
- 2 tsp. soy sauce

Combine venison, bread crumbs, egg, onion and garlic.
Form mixture into balls and fry in oil until brown. Remove
from heat. Combine soup, vinegar, tomatoes, sugar and soy
sauce in pan. Simmer for 20 minutes. Add meatballs,
remove from heat and serve.

Herman Riley
Califon, New Jersey

Hunting Tip ...

*In searching for big, mature bucks, look for rubs on
saplings or small trees. Try to find fresh rubs which
are in open areas, often near scrapes.*

Crockpot Barbecue Venison

Serves: 6-8
Prep Time: 9-11 hours

venison (enough to fill pot)
$1/4$ cup vinegar
$3/4$ cup water
$1/4$ cup Worcestershire sauce
2 cups barbecue sauce

Barbecue Sauce:
1 T. creamstyle horseradish
$1/2$ cup packed brown sugar
$1/2$ cup vinegar
1 T. Worcestershire sauce
1 T. celery seed
2 medium onions, sliced
$1/2$ tsp. salt
$1/2$ cup water
dash pepper

Fill Crockpot with venison. Pour water and vinegar over meat. Pour Worcestershire sauce over mixture and cook on low setting for 8-10 hours. Meanwhile, to prepare barbecue sauce, combine all barbecue sauce ingredients in 3-qt. saucepan. Simmer for 30 minutes on top of stove; set aside. Drain excess liquid and bones from Crockpot. Add barbecue sauce and cook on low setting for another hour.

Noel Garrett
Gambrills, Maryland

Barbecued Deer Ribs

Serves: 4-6
Prep Time: 2 hours

> 3 lbs. venison
> 1 handful hickory and/or mesquite chips
> 1 bottle barbecue sauce
> 2 T. brown sugar
> 2 T. liquid smoke
> 1/4 tsp. onion powder
> 1/4 tsp. garlic powder
> vegetable oil

Presoak hickory or mesquite chips in water for 30 minutes. In large saucepan, add barbecue sauce, brown sugar, liquid smoke and onion and garlic powders. Simmer, stirring frequently over low fire until thickened, approximately 45 minutes to 1 hour. Let cool. Cut ribs along bone. Rub ribs with vegetable oil. Cook ribs on barbecue grill until brown. Brush barbecue sauce on both sides of ribs. Let ribs remain on grill for 15-20 minutes. Remove and serve with your choice of salad and/or side dish.

David Zemba
Cleveland, Ohio

Hunting Tip ...

Waterfowl hunters believe quarry-imitating decoys that have movement abilities often work better in luring gun-shy ducks or geese to the area.

Hunters' Venison

Serves: 6-8, depending on size of loin
Prep Time: 12-24 hours

1 whole venison loin, cut into steaks
   16-oz. beer
   32-oz. tomato paste
6 oz. water
1 T. oregano
2 T. onion, ground

Combine liquid and dry ingredients in large glass bowl to form marinade. Add venison steaks to marinade, making sure each is covered thoroughly. Place in refrigerator for 12-24 hours. Barbecue steaks over medium coals covered with your favorite wood chips.

J. Noble Snowdeal
Bangor, Maine

Did You Know ...

Nearly one-third of the hunters who shoot at targets do so to improve their shooting skills. Other target shooters think it's a great opportunity, and some shoot because they enjoy it as a sport. Some hunters were spurred to shoot at targets because of increased publicity ... or they joined a gun club.

Venison Loaf

Serves: 10
Prep Time: 2 hours

- 2 lbs. ground venison
- 2 lbs. bulk pork sausage
- 2 medium onions, finely chopped
- 1^1/2 cups soda cracker crumbs
- 1 cup evaporated milk
- 3 eggs, lightly beaten
- 1 tsp. salt
- ^{1}/2 tsp. pepper, freshly ground
- 2 cups barbecue sauce (see below)

Barbecue Sauce:
- 1 tsp. salt
- 1 tsp. chili powder
- ^{1}/4 cup brown sugar
- 1 cup tomato sauce
- ^{1}/4 cup vinegar
- 1 onion, finely chopped
- ^{1}/4 cup Worcestershire sauce
- 1 tsp. celery seed
- 2 cups water

Preheat oven to 350 degrees. To make barbecue sauce, combine all sauce ingredients and simmer for 30 minutes. Blend well. Chill for 15 minutes. Place venison, sausage, onion and crumbs in large bowl and mix well. Add milk, eggs, salt, pepper and 1 cup barbecue sauce. Shape into 2 loaves. Place loaves in large, greased baking pans. Bake for 30 minutes. Spoon remaining barbecue sauce over loaves and bake for another 45 minutes.

C.R. Ferrell
Wilson, North Carolina

Venison Muffin Meat Loaf

Serves: 6
Prep Time: 45 minutes

1	lb. ground venison
1	lb. ground pork
2¹/₂	cups bread crumbs
1	cup milk
2	eggs
1	tsp. Worcestershire sauce
1	tsp. liquid smoke
2	tsp. salt
1	tsp. Accent
1	onion, chopped
¹/₂	tsp. pepper
1	tsp. garlic powder
¹/₂	cup brown sugar
¹/₂	cup catsup

Grease muffin pan. Preheat oven to 350 degrees. Combine and mix remaining ingredients. Mix brown sugar and catsup together for topping and set aside. Divide meat mixture into equal portions. Place one in each muffin cup. Before putting pan into oven, spoon topping over each muffin. Bake for 20 minutes.

Joe King
Burleson, Texas

Hunter's Ethics ...

Obey all game laws and regulations. You should also insist that your hunting companions do likewise.

Deer Meat Loaf With Sauce

Serves: 4
Prep Time: 2 hours, 15 minutes

- 1 lb. ground venison
- 1/4 cup shredded cheddar cheese
- 1 small onion, finely chopped
- 1/4 cup green onion, finely chopped
- 1 egg
- 5 bread slices, diced
- 1/2 cup milk
- 1 tsp. Worcestershire sauce
- 1 tsp. minced garlic
- 2 T. cooking oil

Sauce:
- 1 medium onion, diced
- 1/4 cup catsup
- 1 T. vinegar
- 1 tsp. sugar
- 1/2 cup water

Combine all ingredients in large bowl. With fingertips, mix ingredients for 5-10 minutes or until mixture sticks together. Shape into loaf and place in bread pan. Bake for 1-1 1/2 hours at 325-350 degrees. While meat loaf is baking, combine ingredients for sauce in small saucepan and bring to a boil. Cover saucepan and simmer for 10 minutes. Pour over baked meat loaf.

Vivian Poyer
Rock Cave, West Virginia

Venison With Sauerkraut 'n Apples

Serves: 6
Prep Time: 1 hour

2	lbs. ground venison		catsup
1	cup cracker crumbs	1	onion, chopped
1	T. thyme	1	16-oz. can apple pie
1/2	tsp. salt		filling
1/4	tsp. pepper	1	16-oz. can sauerkraut
1	egg, beaten	1	tsp. sugar
1/4	tsp. vinegar		

Combine all ingredients, except pie filing, sauerkraut and sugar. Keep adding catsup until desired thickness. Bake for 30-35 minutes at 350 degrees. In two separate pans, heat apple pie filling (or cook raw apples with sugar) and sauerkraut with sugar. Heap kraut over meat loaf and put apples on top of kraut. Serve warm.

James Knight
Marion, Indiana

Tim's Italian Venison

Serves: varies
Prep Time: overnight plus 1 hour

	venison steaks
1	bottle creamy Italian salad dressing
	Italian-flavored bread crumbs
1/4	lb. butter
	garlic powder to taste
1	tsp. parsley

Marinate venison overnight in salad dressing. Dredge meat in bread crumbs to coat. Melt butter and add garlic powder and parsley. Spread butter mixture over breaded meat. Cover and bake at 400 degrees for 40 minutes.

Tim Fogarty
Westland, Michigan

Sportsman's Marinated Venison

Serves: several
Prep Time: 12-20 hours plus 20-30 minutes

10 lbs. venison, cut into 3/4-inch-thick steaks
1   6-oz. bottle soy sauce
1   10-oz. bottle Italian dressing
1   garlic clove, chopped
1   2-liter-bottle 7-Up soda
1   small can crushed pineapple

In large bowl, combine soy sauce, Italian dressing and garlic to form marinade. Place venison steaks in bowl, making sure they don't touch each other. Pour in 7-Up soda and add pineapple. Marinate for 12-20 hours. Grill meat over open fire until center of meat is hot.

Bill Hardee
Norfolk, Virginia

Marinated Steaks

Serves: varies
Prep Time: 2 hours, 30 minutes

venison steaks
1   tsp. salt
1/4 tsp. pepper
1/4 tsp. basil
1/4 tsp. rosemary
1   T. minced onion (dry)

2   T. salad oil
1   T. wine vinegar

Mix ingredients, except steaks, in shallow pan to form marinade. Add venison steaks and marinate for at least 2 hours, turning occasionally. Broil or grill for about 4 minutes on each side.

John O'Brien
Paradise, California

Grilled Venison In Marinade

Serves: varies
Prep Time: overnight plus 20 minutes

2 lbs. venison steaks
1 cup Balsamic vinegar
3 cups oil
4 garlic cloves
1 T. rosemary
1 T. thyme

Combine ingredients to form marinade and marinate steaks overnight. Grill.

Ray Harrington
Sunrise, Florida

Pan-Fried Venison Steaks

Serves: varies
Prep Time: 30 minutes

1 lb. venison steaks, sliced 1/2 inch thick
1/4 cup thick cream or evaporated milk
1/4 cup flour
3 T. butter or margarine
   salt, pepper and garlic salt to taste

Pound steaks and cut into serving-sized pieces. Dip pieces in cream or milk, dredge in flour and brown one side in hot butter or margarine. Turn. Season with salt, pepper and garlic salt. Brown second side well.

John O'Brien
Paradise, California

Fried Venison Tenderloin Steak

Serves: 6-8
Prep Time: 2 hours

- 6-8 tenderloin steaks, sliced 1/4 inch thick
- 4 cups water
- 2 T. black pepper
- 4 T. garlic salt
- 1 T. baking soda
- 1/4 cup Worcestershire sauce
- 1 cup flour
- 2 cups cooking oil

In medium bowl, mix water, black pepper, garlic salt, baking soda and Worcestershire sauce. Add steaks, cover and let stand at room temperature for 1 hour, 30 minutes. Drain steaks. In large plastic bag, add flour and remaining dry ingredients. Shake to mix. Add steaks and shake until well coated. Preheat oil in frying pan on medium-high heat. When oil is hot, add steaks. Cover and fry for 6-8 minutes. Turn. Do not cover. Fry for 6-8 minutes more or until browned. Drain on paper towels.

Randy White
Lakeside, California

Hunter's Safety ...

You should always keep a gun's muzzle pointed in a safe direction. This will help prevent accidents that sometimes are waiting to happen.

Mushroom-Horseradish Tenderloins

Serves: 2
Prep Time: 30 minutes

> 2 tenderloin steaks, sliced into strips
> 4 T. butter or margarine
> 1 cup fresh mushrooms, sliced
> 2 T. horseradish
> 1 T. spicy brown mustard
> 1 cup water
> 2 T. cornstarch

In large skillet, melt 2 T. butter or margarine and fry tenderloin strips for 10-15 minutes or until tender. In small saucepan, melt 2 T. butter or margarine over medium heat; add mushrooms and saute until tender. Stir in horseradish and mustard. Add water and cornstarch. Bring to a boil, stirring constantly. Then simmer over low heat until thickened. Pour over venison and serve.

Vivian Poyer
Rock Cave, West Virginia

Hunting Tip ...

When you're in or next to a hunting area, move quietly and avoid talking. Use hand signals to communicate. Remember most game animals have excellent hearing and eyesight.

Dutch-Fried Butterflies

Serves: varies
Prep Time: 15 minutes

      butterflied venison loin steaks
      garlic salt
  2 eggs
 1/4 cup milk
      plain bread crumbs
 1-2 onions, sliced into 1/4-inch pieces
      bacon fat
      salt and pepper to taste

Trim all fat from meat. Rinse steaks and pat dry with paper towel. Generously sprinkle garlic salt over steaks. Mix eggs and milk together. Dip steaks into egg mixture and coat with bread crumbs. Cover bottom of large skillet with bacon fat. Fry steaks for 2 minutes, seasoning with salt and pepper. Lower heat and turn steaks over. Put onions on top of steaks and cook for 10 minutes. Remove steaks, leaving onions to finish frying.

Russell Ziegler
Point of Rocks, Maryland

Hunting Tip ...

Trailing wounded game after dark is extremely difficult and can be dangerous, too. Be sure the blood trail is flagged and use a marker to indicate where you stopped; return at daybreak to resume the search.

Grilled Venison Tenderloin

Serves: varies
Prep Time: 4 hours

venison tenderloins
Worcestershire sauce
soy sauce
1 cup white beans
1 cup macaroni
1 T. butter or margarine
1 T. dried parsley, chopped
salt and pepper to taste

Marinate tenderloins in Worcestershire and soy sauce for at least 4 hours then cook on slow grill until done. Cook beans and macaroni in separate pots until done. Combine cooked beans and macaroni with butter, parsley and salt and pepper. Serve with grilled tenderloins.

J.B. Willoughby
Bedford, Indiana

Hunting Tip ...

Use a compass when you're hunting in unfamiliar territory, especially when working in rugged terrain. Everything can soon look the same, which can result in lost hunters.

Dan's Venison Steaks

Serves: varies
Prep Time: 2 days

	venison steaks
2	cups red wine
1/2	cup olive oil
2	yellow onions, sliced
1	carrot, sliced
2	garlic cloves, minced
1/2	tsp. basil
2	bay leaves
10	whole black peppercorns
1	tsp. salt
1	small can sliced mushrooms, drained
1	T. apricot jam
	flour

Combine ingredients (except venison, mushrooms, jam and flour) to form marinade. Marinate steaks for at least 2 days in refrigerator. Remove venison and drain well. Cook meat in hot frying pan for about 10 minutes per side, depending on thickness of steaks. For sauce, heat leftover marinade, adding mushrooms and apricot jam. Thicken sauce with flour and pour sauce over venison. Serve.

Dan Murrell
Indianola, Mississippi

Did You Know ...

Between 34 and 39 percent of hunters enjoy trap-shooting or skeet shooting.

Venison Swiss Steak

Serves: 4
Prep Time: 3 hours

$1^1/_2$ lbs. venison steak, 1-1$^1/_2$ inches thick
  flour
  cooking oil
$1^1/_2$ cups tomato sauce
  1 cup water
  1 medium onion, diced
 $^1/_3$ cup burgundy or red wine
  1 cup carrots, diced (optional)
  1 cup celery, diced (optional)
  salt and pepper to taste

Dredge meat in flour. Brown meat slowly in hot oil for 10 minutes per side. Add tomato sauce and water to cover steaks. Add onion and burgundy. Simmer over low heat for 2-3 hours until meat is tender. Add carrots and celery, if desired, during last hour of cooking. Season with salt and pepper. Serve with fluffy rice or mashed potatoes.

James Warren
Sparks, Nevada

Did You Know ...

More than 80 percent of all hunters have been hunting for at least six years. Of those hunters, more than one-third have hunted for 16 to 20 years, and some have hunted for 41 or more years!

Grilled Venison London Broil

Serves: 2-4
Prep Time: overnight plus 1 hour

    2   large venison steaks, cut London-broil style
        garlic salt
        salt and pepper
  1/4   cup vegetable oil
  1/4   cup vinegar
    2   T. dried onion bits
    1   T. Worcestershire sauce

Slice diagonally 1/4 inch deep and 1 inch across both sides of steaks. Then slice in the other direction, creating diamond-shaped design. Combine oil, vinegar, onion bits and Worcestershire sauce to form marinade and soak steaks overnight. Grill steaks over red coals, searing both sides. Generously season meat with garlic salt and salt and pepper. Reduce heat to low or medium temperature and grill for 8-10 minutes on each side. (Do not overcook.) The inside should be slightly pink (according to your taste) and very juicy. When cooked this way, the true flavor is wonderful. It compares with the best prime rib of beef!

Russell Ziegler
Point of Rocks, Maryland

Hunter's Ethics ...

Obey all the rules of safe gun-handling. You should also courteously but firmly insist that other hunters do the same.

Venison Cube Steak

Serves: 4
Prep Time: 45 minutes

>   4   venison steaks, sliced 1/2 inch thick
>   flour
>   2   cans cream of mushroom soup
>   2   whole carrots, peeled

Pound steaks with meat mallet until thin. Sprinkle flour on
both sides of meat. Wrap 1/2 carrot in each steak and secure
with toothpicks. Brown outside of meat in skillet. Put in
baking dish and cover with mushroom soup. Bake at 350
degrees for 20-25 minutes.

Doug Lynn
Merritt Island, Florida

Smoked Deer Shoulder

Serves: several
Prep Time: overnight plus 2 hours

>   6   lbs. venison shoulder
>   1/2   cup vinegar
>   water
>   1   pkg. dry onion soup mix
>   your favorite seasoning
>   garlic powder to taste
>   3-4   bacon strips

Soak meat overnight in vinegar and water. Drain and make
1/4-inch-deep crosscut in meat. Sprinkle soup mix over meat
and add seasonings as desired. Place bacon strips on meat.
Cook in smoker until done.

John Milton
Lake Wales, Florida

Mark's Venison Steak

Serves: 6-8
Prep Time: 4-6 hours plus 30 minutes

    5   lbs. venison steaks
    1   cup barbecue sauce
    1/3 cup Worcestershire sauce
    1/4 cup soy sauce
    1   tsp. garlic salt
    1   T. Morton Tender Quick
    1   tsp. black pepper
    2   T. Lawry's seasoned salt
    3   eggs
    2   cups cornflake crumbs
    2   T. garlic powder
    2   T. dry onion flakes

Combine barbecue sauce, Worcestershire sauce, soy sauce, garlic salt, Morton's Tender Quick, pepper and 1 T. Lawry's salt to form marinade. Pour over steaks and marinate for 4-6 hours. Remove and dry meat with paper towel. Mix eggs in pie pan. Place each steak in egg mixture. Combine 1 T. Lawry's salt, cornflakes, garlic powder and onion flakes. Dip each steak in cornflake mixture and fry meat as desired.

Mark Outman
Harrison, Michigan

Did You Know ...

NAHC Members average 31 days of hunting a year, and 80,000 Members hunt 60 or more days a year.

Braised Venison—Buffalo Style

Serves: several
Prep Time: 2 hours, 30 minutes

> venison, cut into bite-sized pieces
> cooking oil
> wheat flour
> salt and pepper to taste
> dried green bell pepper (optional)
> dried minced onions (optional)
> dash of tomato paste

$1/4$ cup water

Dredge venison pieces in flour. Heat $1/4$-inch cooking oil in skillet and brown venison slowly, adding seasonings, tomato paste and water. Cover and cook over low heat for 1 hour, 30 minutes or until tender. Add more water, if necessary, to keep meat from scorching.

James Deperto
Buffalo, New York

Did You Know ...

More than two-thirds of all hunters own two or more shotguns, and about one-fourth of those hunters have five or more shotguns. The hunters who own the most shotguns are between the ages of 35 and 54, have average incomes of $55,000 and live in the western part of the country.

Rollups

Serves: 4
Prep Time: 2 hours, 30 minutes

4	venison steaks, cut into 6-inch slices
4	bacon strips
4	small whole onions, peeled
2	T. oil
1	can French onion soup
$1/2$	can water
2	T. catsup
	salt and pepper to taste
4	potatoes, sliced
	flour

Wrap bacon around onion and place on center of steak.
Fold up steak corners and tuck in so onion is totally
enclosed. Wrap with string to secure. Repeat for all four
steaks. Place in cast-iron frying pan with oil. Brown on all
sides (approximately 5-10 minutes).

Combine French onion soup, water, catsup and salt and
pepper; add to pan. Cover and cook on low heat for 90 minutes. Add sliced potatoes arranged around sides. Cover and
cook until potatoes are tender. Remove potatoes and
rollups. Add sufficient flour to make gravy, adding water if
necessary. Remember to cut the string!

Kurt Bramer
Lakeville, Massachusetts

Venison Roll

Serves: 4
Prep Time: 2 hours

1¹/₄ lbs. venison steaks, cut into thin slices
  1 garlic clove, minced
¹/₃ cup grated Parmesan cheese
¹/₃ cup minced parsley
  1 cup soft bread crumbs
¹/₂ tsp. salt
¹/₄ tsp. black pepper
¹/₄ cup pine nuts (optional)
  2 T. olive oil
  1 14-oz. can whole tomatoes (with liquid)
  2 T. tomato paste
¹/₂ tsp. dried thyme, crushed
¹/₂ tsp. dried basil, crushed

Between two sheets of waxed paper, pound each meat slice as thin as possible (use meat mallet, heavy skillet or rolling pin). In medium-sized bowl, mix garlic, cheese, parsley, bread crumbs, salt, pepper and pine nuts. Spread mixture on meat slices, dividing evenly. Roll up each piece and secure with toothpicks or string.

In large frying pan, heat olive oil. Add rolled meat and brown on all sides (6-8 minutes). Add mixture of tomatoes, tomato paste, thyme and basil and bring to a boil. Reduce heat to low. Cover and simmer for 1¹/₄ to 1¹/₂ hours or until rolls are fork-tender. Remove from dish and serve.

Mark Pritt
Manassas, Virginia

'Foiled Again' Venison

Serves: 4
Prep Time: 1 hour, 15 minutes

> 4 venison steaks, sliced 3/4 inch thick
> 4 bacon strips
> 4 small whole onions, peeled
> 1 tomato, sliced
> 4 carrots, peeled and cut into 3-inch pieces
> 4 small celery stalks, cut into 3-inch pieces
> 4 medium potatoes
> 4 pats butter
>   salt and pepper to taste

On four, separate 12-inch square pieces of aluminum foil, place bacon strip, venison steak, onion, tomato and potato. Around sides, place carrot pieces and celery stalks. Top with pat of butter and season to taste. Fold corners of foil pieces up and pinch all sides. Turn each foil package upside down on four more foil sheets, enclosing ingredients completely; place on barbecue grill. (Do not place directly over flame.) Cook for approximately 1 hour. Unwrap carefully and enjoy.

Kurt Bramer
Lakeville, Massachusetts

Hunting Tip ...

Mature bucks tend to run close to the ground and they make good use of cover. If a deer is stotting, it most likely is young.

David's Venison Stew

Serves: 4-6
Prep Time: 2-3 hours

1	lb. venison, cubed
2	T. olive oil
3	onions
4	carrots
1	16-oz. can stewed tomatoes
1	can cream of mushroom soup
	salt and pepper to taste
6	potatoes
2	celery stalks
1	16-oz. can butter beans, drained
1	cup water

Brown venison in oil. Cut vegetables into stew-sized chunks. Add ingredients to pot. Cover and cook over low heat until potatoes are tender, stirring occasionally and adding water as needed. (Use Crockpot if desired.) For an extra meaty stew, use more venison.

David Harper
Huntsville, Alabama

Hunting Tip ...

When encountering an animal at short distances, never look the animal in the eye, even if you believe you are adequately camouflaged. Staring at the animal will make it run. Use your peripheral vision.

Venison Stew

Serves: 6
Prep Time: 3 hours

2	lbs. venison, cubed
1	T. vegetable oil
1	medium onion, diced
1	16-oz. can peeled tomatoes (with juice)
1	16-oz. pkg. frozen stir-fry vegetables
1/2	T. parsley
1	tsp. salt
1/2	tsp. pepper

Heat oil in stew pot. Brown venison and onion together. Add enough water to almost cover and bring to boil. Reduce heat, cover tightly and simmer for 2 hours or until tender. Chop tomatoes and add to mixture. Add vegetable mix, parsley, salt and pepper. Bring to a boil again, then reduce heat, cover and simmer for 30 minutes or until vegetables are tender.

C.R. Ferrell
Wilson, North Carolina

Hunter's Safety ...

Always position a firearm securely when traveling. To transport a gun when using public transportation (bus, train or plane), check first with the carrier's agent concerning its regulations.

Andrew's Venison Stew

Serves: 4-6
Prep Time: 8-10 hours

1^{1}/$_{2}$	lbs. venison, cubed	2	onion slices
	flour	3	cups water
6	potatoes, chopped	1	pkg. beef-stew
3	carrots, chopped		seasoning mix

Dredge meat cubes lightly in flour and stir fry until brown. Put meat in Crockpot. Add remaining ingredients. Cook on low heat for 8-10 hours, stirring once every hour.

Andrew Mancuso
Kingwood, West Virginia

Eric's Venison And Chicken Stew

Serves: several
Prep Time: 2 hours, 30 minutes

2	lbs. venison, cubed	2	tsp. oregano
2	lbs. chicken breast, cubed	2	T. lemon juice (fresh)
^{1}/$_{2}$	cup olive oil	1	cup burgundy
1	tsp. garlic, chopped	1	tsp. salt
6	cups tomatoes, peeled and chopped	^{1}/$_{2}$	tsp. black pepper, freshly ground
2	8-oz. cans green chilis (mild)	^{1}/$_{2}$	tsp. white pepper, freshly ground
2	onions, chopped	1	T. Tabasco sauce
2	T. lime juice (fresh)	1	T. cayenne
1	tsp. cumin		pepper sauce

In skillet, brown venison and chicken separately in olive oil with garlic. Place browned meat in 5-qt. pot and add remaining ingredients. Cover and simmer for 2 hours.

Michael Crump
Peachtree City, Georgia

Whitetail Beans And Venison

Serves: 4-6
Prep Time: 1 hour, 20 minutes

1 lb. venison, ground	$1/2$ cup catsup
cooking oil	2 T. vinegar
1 lb. bacon, diced	1 can pork and beans
1 vandalia onion, sliced	1 can kidney beans
$1/2$ cup brown sugar	1 can butter beans

In skillet, brown meat in oil. Drain and put meat in casserole. Add bacon, onion, brown sugar, catsup and vinegar; mix thoroughly. Drain all beans and add to mixture. Bake for 1 hour at 350 degrees.

Turk Tangert
Lancaster, Pennsylvania

Garlic Venison Stew

Serves: 4-5
Prep Time: 1 hour

2 lbs. venison, cut into $1^1/2$-inch servings
2 T. olive or peanut oil
$1/2$ tsp. dried red chili flakes
$1/4$ cup green onions, sliced
6-7 large garlic cloves, peeled and pressed
2 T. soy sauce
1 cup hot water
$1/8$-$1/4$ cup red wine
$1/2$ tsp. pepper

Heat skillet over high heat and add oil. Add chili flakes and onion. Cook for 20-30 seconds. Add venison and cook for 4-5 minutes until meat is brown. Add remaining ingredients. Simmer (covered) for 40-45 minutes, stirring occasionally.

Stan Roesch
Harrisburg, Pennsylvania

Kentucky Stew

Serves: 6-8
Prep Time: 3-4 hours

2¹/₂	lbs. venison roast
2	T. flour
1	T. paprika
1	tsp. chili powder
2	tsp. salt
3	T. oil
2	onions, sliced
1	garlic clove, minced
1	28-oz. can tomatoes, peeled (undrained)
3	T. chili powder
1	T. cinnamon
1	tsp. ground cloves
1	tsp. red pepper, crushed
2	cups potatoes, chopped
2	cups carrots, chopped

Coat venison in mixture of flour, paprika, 1 tsp. chili powder and salt. In large Dutch oven, brown venison in hot oil. Add onion and garlic and cook until soft. Add peeled tomatoes, 3 T. chili powder, cinnamon, ground cloves and red peppers. Cover and simmer for 2 hours. Add potatoes and carrots and cook until vegetables are done, about 45-60 minutes.

Melvin Shannon
Paris, Kentucky

Venison Burger Casserole

Serves: 4
Prep Time: 1 hour, 30 minutes

   1   lb. ground venison
2^1/$_2$ cups noodles, uncooked
   2   small cans tomato sauce
   1   T. chili powder
   1   onion, chopped
   1   can creamed corn
       cheddar cheese, grated

Combine all ingredients, except cheese; mix thoroughly. Bake for 45-60 minutes. Add cheddar cheese during last 15 minutes.

John O'Brien
Paradise, California

Macaroni And Cheese With Venison Burger

Serves: 4
Prep Time: 1 hour

   1   lb. ground venison
   1   small onion, chopped
   1   pkg. macaroni and cheese (powdered cheese)
   1   pkg. frozen broccoli/cauliflower mix
       margarine
       milk
   1   can sliced mushrooms

Brown meat and onion in large frying pan. While meat mixture is browning, cook macaroni and frozen vegetables together until tender; drain. When meat is brown, melt margarine and add milk and cheese sauce (from macaroni and cheese package directions) to meat mixture. Add mushrooms. Stir until smooth and heat thoroughly. Add macaroni and vegetables to meat mixture; stir.

Karen Bussard
Felton, Pennsylvania

Potato-Topped Venison Casserole

Serves: 6
Prep Time: 1 hour

1 lb. ground venison
cooking oil
2 cups mixed vegetables
1 can cream of celery
or mushroom soup

cheddar cheese, grated
1 box dried potatoes or
2 cups mashed potatoes

Brown venison in oil and remove fat. Put meat in 9-inch-square baking dish. Place vegetables over meat. Spread soup on top of vegetables. Sprinkle with cheese, and top with potatoes. Bake for 45 minutes at 350 degrees.

Steve Coe
Admire, Kansas

Rigatoni Stuffed With Venison

Serves: 6-8
Prep Time: 1 hour, 30 minutes

2 lbs. ground venison
1/2 lb. beef suet
1 tsp. rosemary leaves,
crushed
1/4 tsp. thyme
1/4 tsp. nutmeg
1 garlic clove, crushed
1 tsp. green onion, chopped

1 small onion, chopped
salt and pepper
1/2 lb. rigatoni
longhorn or cheddar
cheese slices
2 small cans Italian-style
tomato sauce
water

In large mixing bowl, combine all ingredients (except rigatoni, cheese and tomato sauce). Cook rigatoni according to directions on package, drain and cool. Stuff rigatoni with meat mixture, place in baking dish and cover with cheese slices. Dilute tomato sauce with equal amount of water and pour over rigatoni mixture. Bake at 350 degrees for 15 minutes, then at 275 degrees for 30 minutes.

Larry Houska
McAlister, Montana

Venison In Wine

Serves: 6
Prep Time: 4 hours

     3   lbs. venison, cut into 1-inch cubes
     2   bay leaves
     1   can cream of mushroom soup
     1   can French onion soup
    3/4 cup dry red wine
     1   8-oz. can sliced mushrooms
    1/4 cup brandy

Combine all ingredients, except brandy, in large casserole. Cover and bake for 3 hours, 30 minutes at 350 degrees. Add brandy and bake for 30 more minutes. Serve on rice, mashed potatoes or egg noodles.

Dan Sowieja
Milwaukee, Wisconsin

Venison Paprika Burgundy

Serves: 6-8
Prep Time: 2 hours

    3¹/₂ lbs. venison
          flour
          oil
      1   T. paprika
      1   can consomme, condensed
          burgundy

Cut venison into chunks, roll in flour, sear in oil and sprinkle with paprika. Add condensed consomme and enough burgundy to cover meat. Cook on low heat for 2 hours. Serve on noodles.

Taj Uhde
Enumclaw, Washington

Venison Stroganoff

Serves: 4-6
Prep Time: 1 hour, 30 minutes

- 2 lbs. venison round steak
- 2 medium onions, diced
- 1/4 cup butter or margarine
- 3 cans tomato soup
- 1/4 cup brown sugar
- 3 6-oz. cans mushrooms
- 2 T. mustard
  Worcestershire sauce
  salt and pepper to taste
- 1 pt. sour cream

Saute onions in butter or margarine. Brown meat in separate pan. Add tomato soup (rinse out can with 1/2-1 cup water), brown sugar, onions, mushrooms and mustard to meat. Cook slowly for 1 hour. Season with Worcestershire sauce and salt and pepper. Add sour cream and cook for 15 more minutes. Serve over noodles or rice. (Add more brown sugar and mustard if desired.)

Gary Ball
Warrens, Wisconsin

Hunter's Safety ...

You should use the right ammunition for your firearm. Carry only one type of ammo in the field to be sure you will not mix different types.

Creole Venison

Serves: 6
Prep Time: 2 hours

2	lbs. venison, cut into 3/4-inch strips
1/4	cup flour
2	tsp. salt
2	tsp. paprika
1/2	tsp. ground black pepper
3	T. vegetable oil
1	cup onion, chopped
1/3	cup green pepper, chopped
1	16-oz. can tomatoes
1/2	cup uncooked rice
1/2	cup beef broth (condensed)
1	cup water

Combine flour, salt, paprika and pepper. Dip meat in mixture. Heat oil in large frying pan. Lightly brown onions and green pepper; remove from oil. Brown meat in remaining oil. Cover meat with onions and green pepper. Cut up tomatoes and add their liquid to meat. Sprinkle rice into pan. Add broth and water, mixing thoroughly. Bring to a boil. Lower heat and cover tightly. Simmer for 1 hour, 30 minutes or until meat is tender. Stir occasionally.

John Judd
Mason, Michigan

Did You Know ...

About one-third of all hunters own the land on which they hunt.

Cajun-Style Venison

Serves: 3-4
Prep Time: 1 hour

  1 lb. ground venison
  1 large onion, chopped
  5 T. shortening
  2 tsp. chili powder
  1 tsp. black pepper
  1 16-oz. can red kidney beans
  1 16-oz. can tomatoes
$1/2$ tsp. garlic salt
  3 cups cooked rice

Brown meat and onion in shortening over medium heat. Add remaining ingredients, except rice. Cook on high heat until simmering. Reduce to low heat for 30-45 minutes. Serve over rice.

Robert Beard
Beaufort, South Carolina

Hunter's Safety ...

At home, always assume that anyone who is not trained in the use of firearms will not know how to handle them properly. To prevent accidents, always store firearms and ammunition separately in locked storage units.

Venison Cheese Chowder

Serves: 4-6
Prep Time: 2 hours

1	lb. venison, ground or diced
1	lb. bacon, diced
1	cup onion, minced
1/2	cup celery, diced
3	garlic cloves, minced
1	cup fresh mushrooms, diced or
2	4-oz. cans sliced mushrooms (with liquid)
4	cups potatoes, diced
1	tsp. salt
1	tsp. pepper
1/2	lb. cheddar or jack cheese, grated
1	cup flour
1	qt. milk

Fry bacon in skillet until crisp. Drain and put in soup pot. Brown venison in same skillet, using bacon grease if needed, and put in soup pot. Saute raw vegetables until tender and put in soup pot. Add potatoes, mushrooms, salt and pepper and cover with water. Simmer until potatoes are tender. Coat grated cheese with flour to prevent lumping. When potatoes are done, add milk, cheese/flour, stirring until cheese is melted and chowder is hot. Additional liquid or thickening may be used to adjust consistency. Season to taste and serve.

Lyle Christman
Marysville, Washington

Cabbage And Venison Soup

Serves: 4-6
Prep Time: 1 hour, 15 minutes

1 lb. ground venison	1/2 tsp. garlic powder with parsley
1/2 cup olive oil	
1 tsp. garlic, chopped	1 onion, chopped
1 16-oz. can dark red kidney beans	2 cups water
	1/4 tsp. white pepper
1 28-oz. can chopped tomatoes	1 T. cayenne pepper sauce
2 celery stalks, chopped	4 beef bouillon cubes

In skillet, brown venison with olive oil and garlic over medium heat. Place browned meat in large soup pan or Dutch oven and add remaining ingredients. Slowly bring to a boil. Reduce heat, cover and simmer for 1 hour.

Michael Crump
Peachtree City, Georgia

Crump's Crockpot Chili

Serves: 6-8
Prep Time: 4-6 hours

2 lbs. ground venison, browned	2 T. chili powder
	1/2 T. Tabasco sauce
2 15-oz. cans chili hot beans	2 16-oz. cans chopped tomatoes
1 tsp. cumin	1 tsp. salt
2 whole onions, coarsely chopped	1 tsp. lemon pepper
	1/2 tsp. garlic, freshly chopped
2 whole jalapeno peppers, coarsely chopped	
1/2 T. red-hot cayenne pepper sauce	

Place all ingredients in Crockpot. Stir once, cover and cook for 4-6 hours on high setting.

Michael Crump
Peachtree City, Georgia

Deer Chili

Serves: varies
Prep Time: 1 hour, 15 minutes

> 2 lbs. ground venison
> 3/4 cup green pepper
> 1 medium onion, diced
> 1 tsp. salt
> 1 can chili beans
> 1 10-oz. can diced tomatoes and green chilis
> 2 8-oz. cans tomato sauce
> 1/2 cup catsup
> 1 T. Worcestershire sauce
> 1-2 T. Tabasco sauce
> 1 pkg. chili seasoning

Brown and drain venison, green pepper, onion and salt. Add remaining ingredients and simmer for 1 hour.

Steve Coe
Admire, Kansas

Hunter's Ethics ...

Do your best to acquire the marksmanship and hunting skills required to assure clean, sportsmanlike kills. Practice continuing education to ensure constant learning and fine-tuning.

Smoked Venison Chili

Serves: 6
Prep Time: 2-3 hours

2^1/$_2$ lbs. smoked dried venison (recipe follows on next page)
2-3 T. vegetable oil
2 medium onions, diced
^{1}/$_2$ cup tomato paste
3-4 cups beef or chicken stock
6 garlic cloves, minced
1 T. ground cumin
2-3 T. chili powder
1 T. oregano
salt and pepper to taste
1-2 dried chilis, crushed
1 1-lb. can peeled tomatoes with juice, chopped
2 cans chipotle chilis (or substitute)

Add 1-2 T. oil to large iron skillet; heat to smoking point. Add onions and cook until lightly browned. Add tomato paste and cook slowly with onions until mixture loses its bright red color and appears "rusty." Add stock or water as needed to prevent tomato paste from sticking and burning. Continue cooking over low heat until tomato and onion mixture is brown and all liquid has evaporated. Add remaining oil, garlic and spices. Cook 2-3 more minutes, being careful not to let mixture burn. Transfer mixture to heavy 4- to 6-qt. saucepot or Dutch oven. Add remaining ingredients, except rice. Bring to a boil. Cook over low heat for 2-3 hours, adding stock as needed to moisten dried venison. Serve on lemon cilantro rice (from page 59).

Joseph Kozlowski
Nemacolin, Pennsylvania

Smoked Dried Venison

2-2$^1/_2$ lbs. venison leg meat, boneless
2-3 T. toasted cumin seeds, crushed
$^3/_4$ cup kosher salt or
$^2/_3$ cup table salt
3 T. cracked black pepper

Toast whole cumin seeds over medium-low heat until lightly browned and aromatic. Cool and crush before measuring. Cut venison into $^1/_2$-inch strips. Lay meat on metal rack. Coat lightly with salt, pepper and toasted cumin. Put in oven at 100 degrees for 4-5 hours. When done, meat should be slightly flexible yet not too dry. Finish meat in smoker for 15-20 minutes or grill over hot coals, adding dampened hardwood chips onto coals. Use as ingredient for chili.

Joseph Kozlowski
Nemacolin, Pennsylvania

Lemon Cilantro Rice

1 T. vegetable oil
1 medium onion, minced
1 lemon, remove peel and save
2 cups converted rice
4 cups chicken stock

2 tsp. salt
1 tsp. cracked black pepper
1 lemon (juice)
3-4 T. cilantro, chopped

Heat oil in covered, heavy saucepot. Add onions; cook until translucent. Add lemon peel then rice, stirring to coat with oil. Add stock; bring to a boil. Add salt and pepper. Cover. Reduce to low heat. Cook for 18-20 minutes. Maintain a simmer throughout cooking time and do not stir. When rice is done, squeeze juice from lemon and add cilantro. Fluff gently with fork. Adjust seasonings if needed. Let stand for 4-5 minutes before serving with chili.

Joseph Kozlowski
Nemacolin, Pennsylvania

Venison Loins In Bear Swamp Marinade

Serves: 3-4
Prep Time: overnight plus 20 minutes

- 1 lb. venison loins, thinly sliced
- 3 T. mustard
- 2 T. horseradish
- 1/4 cup oil
- 1 T. dry basil
- 1/4 tsp. black pepper
- 5 dashes Tabasco sauce
- 1 T. garlic, crushed
- 2 T. Worcestershire sauce

Combine all ingredients to form marinade. Marinate loins overnight. Saute loins in frying pan until tender.

Ray Bussnick
Emerson, New Jersey

Larry's Venison Marinade

Serves: varies
Prep Time: 12 hours, 30 minutes

- venison steaks, cut 3/4 inch thick
- 1/2 cup soy sauce
- 1/2 cup Worcestershire sauce
- 1 3/4 cups pineapple juice
- 1/4 cup red wine vinegar
- 1/3 cup sugar
- 1/2 tsp. garlic powder

Combine all ingredients, except venison, to form marinade. Pour over venison and marinate in refrigerator for 12 hours. Drain off marinade. Cook on grill and enjoy!

Larry Lance
Blairsville, Georgia

Hunter's Venison Pie

Serves: 4-6
Prep Time: 1 hour

1-2 lbs. venison roast
1 T. butter
3 onions, diced
1 garlic clove, minced
1 can tomatoes
1 T. paprika
1 pinch cayenne pepper (optional)
1 bay leaf
   dash thyme
1 cup beer
4 potatoes, peeled and quartered
2-3 carrots, sliced
1 cup frozen or canned peas

Biscuit Topping:
1 cup flour
3/4 cup yellow cornmeal
1 T. sugar
1 T. baking powder
3/4 cup milk
3 T. shortening, melted
1 egg, slightly beaten
1/2 tsp. salt

Cut meat into 1-inch squares, removing fat and sinew. Heat butter in skillet and brown meat quickly to retain juices. Add onions, garlic, tomatoes, seasonings, beer, potatoes, carrots and peas. Cover and cook slowly for about 30 minutes until meat is almost tender. Remove from heat and pour into baking dish. Combine biscuit-topping ingredients to form batter. Using spoon, drop batter onto top of meat mixture. Bake at 425 degrees for 25 minutes or until topping is browned.

Mark Pritt
Manassas, Virginia

Venison Pot Roast

Serves: 6-8
Prep Time: 4 hours

3-4 lbs. venison roast
2 large onions, sliced
potatoes, pared and quartered
celery, chopped
carrots, chopped
1 can beer
pepper to taste

Place roast in large roasting pan with onion slices on top. Arrange vegetables around roast. Pour beer over entire roast and season with pepper. Bake at 350 degrees until tender, about 3-4 hours.

Karen Bussard
Felton, Pennsylvania

Did You Know ...

Nearly two-thirds of all centerfire-rifle hunters use different centerfire rifles for different game. For the other third, one centerfire rifle does the job for taking all types of game.

Deer Pot Roast

Serves: varies
Prep Time: 3 hours, 30 minutes

4	lbs. venison round or hind leg roast
2	garlic cloves, crushed
2	large onions, diced
2	T. Worcestershire sauce
4	tsp. salt
1	tsp. sugar
1/4	tsp. cracked pepper
	water
8	medium carrots, chunked
8	new potatoes, chunked

Place venison roast in Dutch oven. Insert garlic into roast and bind with string. Add onions, Worcestershire sauce, salt, sugar, pepper and water. Cover and bake at 350 degrees for 2 hours. Add carrots and potatoes and continue baking 1-1 1/2 hours, turning meat occasionally. Transfer to platter. Remove strings and discard. With slotted spoon, arrange vegetables around meat. Serve with liquid over meat and vegetables.

Jeff Tenhundfeld
Germantown, Tennessee

Hunting Tip ...

When drawing a bow on game, try to use very little motion. If possible, wait until the animal's view is blocked by a tree or bush to draw your bow.

Jack's Pot Roast

Serves: 12
Prep Time: 2 hours, 30 minutes

5	lbs. venison rump roast
4	T. vegetable or olive oil
1	T. salt
1	T. pepper
2	whole cloves
1	large onion (whole)
1	T. basil
1	T. thyme
1	bay leaf
5	garlic cloves, crushed
2	large onions, sliced
1¹/₂	cups beef broth
5	Roma tomatoes (whole)
3	T. tomato paste

Heat oil until hot in Dutch oven or large skillet. Season meat with salt and pepper. Slowly brown meat for 10-15 minutes. Insert whole cloves in whole onion. Add all ingredients to meat; cover meat with sheet of oiled waxed paper to keep moist. Cover and cook on low heat for 1 hour, 30 minutes or until done. Transfer meat to large platter. Skim fat from gravy and discard. Pour gravy through sieve, pressing vegetables through sieve to thicken gravy.

Jack Barnes
Dallas, Texas

Venison Wine Roast

Serves: 4
Prep Time: 10 hours

  1   3-5 lb. shoulder roast
  1   cup blush wine
$1/4$ cup V-8 juice
$1/2$ tsp. basil, crushed
$3/4$ cup Worcestershire sauce
  2   large onions, chopped
3-4 carrots, cut into 1-inch sections
3-4 small potatoes, quartered

In plastic bag, combine wine, V-8 juice, basil and Worcestershire sauce. Add meat and seal bag; marinate in refrigerator for 4-6 hours. Place roast in roasting pan and add onions, carrots and potatoes. Bake for 3 hours, 30 minutes at 300 degrees.

Andrew Lennox
East Greenville, Pennsylvania

Did You Know ...

More than one-third of all hunters reload their own ammunition. Of those who reload, 61 percent reload their own shotshells. Some 65 percent reload center-fire rifle cartridges.

Grilled Venison Roast

Serves: 4-8
Prep Time: 6 hours, 30 minutes

1	2-4 lb. rump or loin roast
1/2	cup vegetable oil
1/2	small onion, chopped
1/2	T. Worcestershire sauce
1	tsp. Morton Nature's Seasons
1	tsp. Mrs. Dash (original blend)
1/2	tsp. salt
1/4	tsp. pepper

In large bowl, combine ingredients. Add roast. (Make sure to cover roast completely with marinade.) Cover bowl and marinate in refrigerator for 2-4 hours, turning roast periodically. Remove roast and cook slowly on covered grill for 2 hours, 30 minutes or until done. Heat marinade in saucepan, adding water to thin. Baste roast with marinade when turning. (Tips: Cook with chicken for added drippings; add a chunk of wet hickory for more smoke flavor.)

John Richardson
Springfield, Illinois

Did You Know ...

About 18 percent of all hunters purchase reloaded ammo, rather than reloading themselves. Most buy the reloaded ammo from a retail outlet, although one third of those using purchased reloads get them from a friend.

Broiled Venison Chops

Serves: 4-6
Prep Time: 20 minutes

  4-6 venison chops, sliced 1/2 inch thick
    1 pinch seasoning salt
    1 pinch garlic powder
    1 pinch cayenne pepper (optional)

Season chops with seasoning salt, garlic powder and cayenne pepper. Broil chops 4-6 inches from heat for 6-8 minutes. Turn and continue broiling until done.

Randy White
Lakeside, California

Great Grilled Burgers

Serves: 4
Prep Time: 30-45 minutes

  1 lb. ground venison
  1 T. garlic salt
  1 T. black pepper
  1 tsp. chili powder (optional)
  2 T. Worcestershire sauce

Glaze (optional):
  1/2 cup catsup
    2 T. Worcestershire sauce
  1/2 tsp. mustard
    1 T. brown sugar

Combine venison with all ingredients, except glaze, and shape into 4 patties. In separate bowl, combine glaze ingredients. Spray rack with non-stick coating. Grill over hot coals until done, applying glaze occasionally.

Randy White
Lakeside, California

Venison Barbecued Burgers

Serves: 4
Prep Time: 45 minutes

  1 lb. ground venison
2/3 cup onion, chopped
  2 T. oil
1/4 cup water
  1 can chicken gumbo soup
  1 T. mustard
1/2 tsp. salt
1/2 tsp. pepper
  2 T. catsup

Cook venison and onion in oil until browned, turning frequently. Add remaining ingredients and simmer for 30 minutes on low heat, stirring occasionally.

Mike Neilson
Danville, Indiana

Did You Know ...

Over 80 percent of hunters own centerfire rifles while two-thirds own at least one rimfire rifle. Twenty-nine percent of all hunters own at least one black-powder rifle. Those who own the most centerfire rifles are at least 55 years old, have average incomes of $55,000 and live in the West.

Rainy-Day Barbecued Deerburgers

Serves: 4
Prep Time: 30 minutes

> 1 lb. ground venison
> 1/2 cup raisin bran cereal
> 1 tsp. salt
> 1/2 cup milk
> 1 egg
> 1/2 cup onions, chopped
> 1 cup catsup
> 1/4 cup vinegar
> 1/4 cup water
> 2 T. brown sugar
> 1 T. dry mustard

Combine meat, raisin bran, salt, milk and egg; form into patties. Brown patties in deep skillet. Add onions. Mix remaining ingredients and add to skillet when onions are browned. Cover and simmer for 10-15 minutes.

Blaise Lacaprucia
South Windsor, Connecticut

Did You Know ...

Four out of five NAHC Members hunt big game. Of that number, 76 percent hunt white-tailed deer. Hunters of mule deer and other deer make up the next largest category at 22 percent.

Quick Venison Patties

Serves: 6-8
Prep Time: 20 minutes

     1   lb. ground venison
     1   lb. pork sausage
    1/4 cup Grueyere or Swiss cheese, grated
         salt and pepper to taste

Place venison and pork sausage in large bowl. Add grated cheese and season with salt and pepper. Lightly mix all ingredients. Pan-fry over medium heat for 15 minutes.

Bruce Bitterman
Bismarck, North Dakota

Did You Know ...

The following are the top five reasons why hunters go shooting, according to a shooting industry study:
  1. A friend calls and invites you to go hunting
  2. You have a free day's shooting at a club
  3. An opportunity arises for trying something new in shooting
  4. There is a chance of winning cash prizes in a shooting event
  5. You just watched a TV program about hunting

Tender Venison Kabobs

Serves: 4-6
Prep Time: 4-24 hours

    2   lbs. venison, cubed
$1/3$ cup soy sauce
$1/4$ cup oil
$1/4$ cup sherry
$1/4$ cup green onions, sliced
    1   T. ginger, chopped
    1   T. sesame seeds
    1   T. sugar
    3   garlic cloves, crushed
        dash Tabasco

Combine all ingredients and pour over meat. Refrigerate overnight. Skewer meat kabob-style alone or with mushrooms, onion, peppers and tomatoes. Barbecue kabobs on grill and serve.

Dean Hendrickson
Quartz Hill, California

Did You Know ...

White-tailed deer hunters spend less on equipment, apparel and hunting trips than do waterfowl and upland bird hunters and bowhunters. The most money is spent by waterfowl hunters.

Colorful Venison Stir-Fry

Serves: 6
Prep Time: 1 hour, 15 minutes

1	lb. venison, cubed
1/4	cup cooking oil
1/4	cup soy sauce and water (combined)
2	T. Tabasco sauce
2	T. minced garlic
2	T. steak sauce
2	T. white cooking wine
2	T. Worcestershire sauce
2	T. cooking oil
1/2	cup green peppers, cut into thin strips
1/2	cup red peppers, cut into thin strips
1/2	cup yellow peppers, cut into thin strips
1	cup green onions, cut into 1/2-inch strips
1/2	cup mushrooms, sliced
1	cup tomatoes, diced
1	cup water
3	T. cornstarch

In large bowl, combine cooking oil, soy sauce, water, Tabasco sauce, garlic, steak sauce, white wine and Worcestershire sauce to form marinade. Marinate venison at room temperature for 30 minutes. In wok or large skillet, heat cooking oil. Drain off marinade and add meat to skillet, browning for 10-15 minutes. Remove from pan. Add peppers and onions to pan, cooking for 5 minutes. Add mushrooms and tomatoes and cook until all vegetables are tender. Add venison and stir. In separate pan, combine water and cornstarch. Bring to a boil; cover and simmer until thickened. Add to meat and vegetable mixture, stirring thoroughly. Serve with hot, buttered noodles.

Vivian Poyer
Rock Cave, West Virginia

Quick Venison Jerky

Serves: several
Prep Time: 1 hour

1^1/$_2$ lbs. venison flank steak or rib-eyed steak
^{1}/$_4$ tsp. salt
^{1}/$_4$ tsp. garlic salt
^{1}/$_4$ tsp. black pepper, freshly ground

Cut partially frozen steaks into ^{1}/$_8$-inch strips. Combine spices and sprinkle over meat. Place meat strips on (waxed) paper plates and cover with waxed paper. Microwave at 20-30 percent power (low) for 20 minutes. Remove from microwave; turn meat strips over, season meat again and cook at 20-30 percent power for another 20 minutes. Store in covered container or refrigerate.

Dodman Nobel
Fortville, Indiana

Venison Chew

Serves: several
Prep Time: 2 hours, 30 minutes

1	lb. ground venison	^{1}/$_8$	tsp. garlic powder
3	T. soy sauce	^{1}/$_8$	tsp. onion powder
1	T. Worcestershire sauce	^{1}/$_8$	tsp. salt
^{1}/$_4$	tsp. ground pepper	1	T. liquid smoke
^{1}/$_8$	tsp. allspice	1	T. water

Combine ingredients, except liquid smoke and water. Between two sheets of waxed paper, roll half of meat mixture until ^{1}/$_8$ inch thick. Remove top sheet and flip meat slab onto cookie sheet. Remove waxed paper. Repeat procedure with remaining meat mixture. Brush meat with liquid smoke and water. Bake at 200-225 degrees for 1 hour until brown. Turn over for another hour or until desired texture.

Herman Riley
Califon, New Jersey

Deer Stix

Serves: several
Prep Time: 3 days plus 7 hours

3	lbs. ground venison	3	tsp. garlic salt
2	lbs. ground chuck	3	tsp. hickory smoke salt
4	tsp. mustard seed	1	tsp. red pepper, crushed
4	tsp. cracked pepper	5	tsp. Morton Tender Quick

Combine all spices in metal or glass bowl. Sprinkle spices over chuck and venison, mixing well. Cover and place in refrigerator for 3 days, stirring thoroughly once a day. After third day, divide into 5 portions (1 lb. each), roll into logs and place on rack of broiler pan. Bake for 7 hours at 200 degrees.

Jeff Dolick
San Antonio, Texas

Italian-Style Venison Liver

Serves: several
Prep Time: 20 minutes

> venison liver, sliced
> onions, chopped
> butter
2 cups tomato sauce
> tarragon, basil, oregano to taste
> salt, pepper, garlic to taste
> red wine

Saute liver and onions in butter for 5-10 minutes. Add tomato sauce, spices and wine. Simmer on low heat until done. Serve.

Blaise Lacaprucia
South Windsor, Connecticut

Venison Sausage

Serves: varies
Prep Time: 9 hours

5   lbs. venison burger
2   T. meat-cure salt
2   tsp. mustard seed
2   tsp. coarse black pepper
1   T. garlic salt
1   tsp. hickory smoked salt

Combine all ingredients, mixing well. Refrigerate in air-tight container for 3 days, removing mixture every day to knead. On fourth day, form 4 rolls, about 14 inches long each. Broil at 175 degrees for 8 hours. Turn rolls over for last 2 hours.

Mark Outman
Harrison, Michigan

Did You Know ...

More than 70 percent of your fellow NAHC Members consider themselves to be advanced or expert hunters. Of course, the more experienced and advanced they become, the more they hunt. They also spend more on hunting gear, apparel, equipment and travel.

Sausage Stuffed Venison

Serves: 8-10
Prep Time: 4-6 hours

8-10 lbs. venison hind quarter
   1 long Polish sausage
      salt and pepper to taste
      garlic salt
   2 cups burgundy

Remove bone from hind quarter of venison. Place Polish sausage in cavity. Season roast with salt and pepper and garlic salt. Place roast in center of large sheet of heavy-duty aluminum foil and add burgundy. Close and fasten foil with double fold; place on baking sheet. Bake at 350 degrees for 4-6 hours. Make gravy with drippings in foil.

Mark Pritt
Manassas, Virginia

Did You Know ...

NAHC's advanced and expert hunters spend an average of $763 on equipment and apparel and $1,307 on hunting trips each year. This is 41 percent more on equipment and apparel than beginners-intermediates; it is more than double for hunting trips.

Venison Stuffed Peppers

Serves: 4-5
Prep Time: 1 hour

    1   lb. venison sausage, ground
    1   egg
    1/2 cup bread crumbs
    1/4 cup green onions, diced
    4   green peppers
    1/2 cup water
        catsup or chili sauce

Combine venison, egg, bread crumbs and onions. Cut green peppers in half, lengthwise, removing seeds. Stuff meat mixture into pepper halves. Put peppers in baking dish and add water. Top peppers with catsup or chili sauce. Cover dish with plastic wrap and microwave for 40-50 minutes.

Bill Schmidt
Clovis, California

Did You Know ...

NAHC Members are good at giving advice. Seventy percent admit to giving friends and neighbors advice about equipment and supplies while 63 percent have been known to share their knowledge of hunting techniques. Over half of these Members have provided tips about good hunting spots.

Stuffed Boiled Venison Log

Serves: varies
Prep Time: 90 minutes

2	lbs. ground venison
1	medium onion, finely chopped
1¹/2	cups rolled oats
4	T. steak sauce
	salt and pepper to taste
8	boiled ham slices
1	lb. shredded mozzarella cheese

Combine all ingredients, except ham and cheese. Put mixture in center of heavy duty aluminum foil. Flatten venison to 12x14-inch slab. Put ham slices, side by side, on top of mixture. Sprinkle cheese over ham. Lift one end of foil and roll meat into log. Pinch each end of log so cheese won't leak out. Place in baking dish and bake at 350 degrees for 30 minutes.

Daniel House
St. Charles, Missouri

Hunting Tip ...

When glassing an area for big game, watch for telltale movements and things that appear to "not belong." These things are often the tips of antlers or parts of a horn.

Stuffed Venison Sausage

Serves: several (yield: 30 sausages)
Prep Time: 1 hour, 30 minutes

    8   lbs. ground venison (lean)
    2   lbs. bacon ends or fatty bacon, chopped
$1/2$ cup salt
    3   T. black pepper
    1   T. mustard seed
    2   T. garlic powder
    1   tsp. onion powder
    3   tsp. sage
$1/2$ cup water

Mix venison and bacon together. Combine all ingredients, mixing thoroughly. Grind through fine plate ($1/8$-inch holes) and stuff casings. Twist or tie into lengths approximately 4 inches long. Heat in 170-degree water until internal temperature reaches 152 degrees. Use meat thermometer to maintain this temperature for 10 minutes. Immediately immerse in ice-cold water; blot dry and refrigerate. Wrap to freeze.

Dodman Nobel
Fortville, Indiana

Did You Know ...

Bowhunters average 11 more days (42) in the field than do their gun-toting-only brethren. While most bowhunting members own at least two bows, they also own 11 firearms, on average.

Trail Bologna

Serves: several
Prep Time: 25 hours

    2   lbs. ground venison
    2   T. meat-cure salt
    2   tsp. mustard seed
    2   tsp. black pepper
    2   tsp. liquid smoke
  1/2   tsp. red pepper
  1/4   tsp garlic powder
  1/8   cup water

Combine all ingredients, cover and refrigerate for 24 hours.
Shape into rolls. Bake for 1 hour at 300 degrees. Let cool.
Refrigerate.

Victor Lenegar
Wellston, Ohio

Did You Know ...

*Most NAHC bowhunters go after white-tailed deer.
Over 76 percent, in fact. Almost as many
bowhunters try to take turkeys as do bowhunters
seeking out other species of deer—about 30,000 for
each. Bear and elk are other popular quarry, and
some 23,500 enjoy bowfishing.*

West Virginia Garlic Heart

Serves: 3-4
Prep Time: 40 minutes

  1   venison heart
 1/4 lb. butter
  2   garlic cloves, minced
      salt to taste
  2   T. pepper
  1   4-oz. can sliced mushrooms

Melt butter and add garlic, salt, pepper and mushrooms.
Place heart in sauce. Bake in covered dish at 350 degrees for
30 minutes. Slice and serve with mushrooms.

Kevin Farley
Beckley, West Virginia

Hunting Tip ...

*Bowhunters should wait 30 minutes or more before
pursuing the big-game animals they have shot. If the
animal isn't fatally wounded, this timeframe allows
it to bed down nearby; otherwise, you will force the
animal to keep moving and you may never find it.*

Boiled Venison Heart

Serves: 1-2
Prep Time: overnight plus 1 hour

1	venison heart, halved lengthwise
1/2	tsp. salt
1/4	tsp. black pepper
2	bay leaves
1/2	tsp. oregano
1/2	tsp. marjoram
	dash nutmeg
2	cups water

Remove all fat and blood from heart and soak in salted water overnight. Combine seasonings and water; boil for 5 minutes to bring out flavor of seasonings. Add heart, cover and boil until heart is tender, approximately 45-50 minutes. Serve with horseradish, mustard and rye bread.

Larry Houska
McAlister, Montana

Hunter's Safety ...

When using a tree stand, you most likely will climb the tree before daylight and come down after dark. You should practice climbing trees in this situation (with any portable tree stand) at home before venturing into the woods.

Venison Heart In Wine

Serves: 1-2
Prep Time: 2 hours, 15 minutes

   1   venison heart
       butter
2-3 cups beef bouillon
2-3 cups red wine

Brown venison heart in butter. In saucepan, cover heart with equal amounts of beef bouillon and red wine. Cover and simmer for about 2 hours. If desired, thicken juices to make gravy. Serve with horseradish and creamed spinach.

Dan Sowieja
Milwaukee, Wisconsin

Did You Know ...

The following are the top five reasons why many hunters go bowhunting:
   1. They like the challenge and the skill required in bowhunting
   2. Longer bow seasons give them more opportunity to hunt
   3. It's a fun sport
   4. Hunting areas generally are less crowded
   5. Bowhunting is different so it provides a change of pace

Venison Mincemeat

Serves: varies
Prep Time: 2 hours

1	lb. ground venison
3³/4	lbs. apples, chopped
1	lb. raisins
1/2	lb. currants
1	T. salt
5	cups brown sugar
3	T. cinnamon
1/2	tsp. cloves
2	tsp. nutmeg
1	tsp. ginger

Combine ingredients and simmer for 2 hours. Pour into pint-sized jars.

Ernest Gassett
Wautoma, Wisconsin

Hunting Tip ...

In cold air, animals can see your breath as easily as you can see theirs. Breathe through your nose. If you have difficulty keeping your nasal passages clear, use a nasal spray.

Canned Venison And Noodles

Serves: 4
Prep Time: 30 minutes

```
1   pt. canned venison
2   cups prepared noodles
2   medium onions, diced
2   T. butter
1/2 cup flour
1/2 cup water
1   tsp. salt
1   tsp. pepper
1/4 tsp. garlic powder
```

Cook noodles and saute onions in butter until done. Combine remaining ingredients, except venison, in bowl or jar. Stir or shake until smooth. Add mixture to canned venison and prepared noodles. Heat thoroughly in pan. Stir frequently and serve.

Dodman Nobel
Fortville, Indiana

Hunting Tip ...

Don't let a light rain or snow spoil your hunting plans. Animals often will forage during these periods. The rain and snow limit the spread of scent and will muffle the sounds you make.

Canned Venison Stroganoff

Serves: 4
Prep Time: 1 hour, 30 minutes

 1 pt. canned venison
 1 large onion, chopped
 2 T. butter
 1 chicken bouillon cube
 1 cup water
 1/4 tsp. salt
 1/4 tsp. pepper
 1 can cream of mushroom soup
 1/2 cup sour cream

Saute onion in butter. Dissolve bouillon cube in water. Add bouillon mixture and remaining ingredients to onion. Heat thoroughly and serve over noodles or rice.

Dodman Nobel
Fortville, Indiana

Deer Liver Pate

Serves: varies
Prep Time: 30 minutes

 venison liver
 red or white wine or cognac
 sour cream
 cream cheese
 sweet basil
 dill weed

Saute liver until brown. Blend liver in food processor with remaining ingredients to form paste. Let cool and refrigerate. Serve with crackers.

T. Sulmeisters
Conifer, Colorado

Venison Orsini

Serves: 6-8
Prep Time: 30 minutes

1-1^1/$_2$ lbs. venison, cut into ^{1}/$_2$-inch cubes
  3-4 garlic cloves, sliced
    4 T. butter
    1 lb. fresh mushrooms, sliced
    1 small yellow onion, sliced
    1 green pepper, sliced
12-16 oz. sour cream
    1 6-oz. bottle oyster sauce
       salt and pepper to taste
    2 loaves French bread (toasted)

In large cast-iron skillet, saute garlic in 1 T. butter over medium heat. Add remaining butter, venison, mushrooms, onion and green pepper. Saute until meat is browned. Reduce heat and cover; cook for approximately 5 minutes. Add sour cream, oyster sauce and seasonings. Cook on low heat for an additional 5 minutes until mixture is thoroughly heated. Serve on toast.

Mark Madison
Cambridge, New York

Hunting Tip ...

Mule deer bucks like to bed in fairly dense cover that offers a good view of their backtrail, approach routes and where wind can reach them.

Venison Burritos

Serves: 6
Prep Time: 30 minutes

> 1   lb. ground venison
> 1   15-oz. can hot chili beans, mashed
> 1¹/2 cups thick and chunky salsa
> 8   flour tortillas
> 1   cup cheddar cheese, shredded
> 1   cup tomatoes, diced
> 1   cup lettuce, chopped into bite-sized pieces
>   sour cream (optional)

Brown venison in skillet. Stir in chili beans and 1 cup salsa. Place ¹/4 cup meat mixture, 2 T. cheddar cheese, 1 T. salsa and tomatoes and lettuce on each tortilla. Fold tortilla envelope-style. Top with sour cream if desired.

Vivian Poyer
Rock Cave, West Virginia

Hunting Tip ...

If cover looks too difficult to hunt and has good escape routes, you'll most likely find deer. If it looks difficult to you, it probably has to other hunters, too. It's most likely a good sanctuary for game animals.

Venison Steak Sandwich

Serves: varies
Prep Time: 30 minutes

> venison steaks
> butter or margarine
> green peppers, sliced into strips
> onions, sliced into strips
> mushrooms, sliced
> Worcestershire sauce
> soy sauce
> buns
> cheese slices

Grill or panfry steaks as desired. In butter or margarine, saute green peppers, onions and mushrooms. Add Worcestershire sauce and soy sauce. Place steak on bun and melt your favorite cheese on top. Top with vegetables.

Gary Ball
Warrens, Wisconsin

Hunting Tip ...

Learn to profit from your misses as well as your hits. Keep a diary and make lots of notations on the conditions, terrain and type of ammunition used— record anything that will improve your chances of success next time.

Smoke-Flavored BBQ Roast Sandwiches

Serves: several
Prep Time: 30-45 minutes

1	venison roast, cooked
1/8	cup butter
1/2	tsp. dry mustard
2	beef bouillon cubes
1/2	tsp. liquid smoke
2	cups water
1/2	cup catsup
1/4	cup brown sugar
1/4	cup Heinz 57 steak sauce
1	garlic clove, minced
	salt and pepper to taste

Grind cooked venison roast and put in large frying pan.
Add remaining ingredients, mixing thoroughly. Cook on
high heat for 5 minutes; reduce heat and simmer until mixture becomes thick. Stir occasionally to prevent sticking.
Serve on bread or buns.

Rodger Nelson
Canton, Illinois

Hunting Tip ...

*If you're planning a guided hunting trip, be sure your
guide knows your strengths and weaknesses as a
hunter before you set out on the hunt. Be sure you're
prepared physically, particularly if you're hunting in
the mountains.*

Venison Rubino

Serves: 4
Prep Time: 1 hour, 30 minutes

    8   venison loin cuts
  1-2   garlic cloves, minced
    1   cup Italian salad dressing
    1   large onion, chopped
    2   small carrots, peeled and chopped
    1   celery stalk, chopped
    1   broccoli stalk, chopped
    1   small cucumber, chopped
         French bread slices

Combine garlic cloves and Italian salad dressing. In 1/2 cup of garlic salad dressing, marinate loin cuts for 1 hour. Pour remaining salad dressing over prepared vegetables. Saute each side of loins on medium-high heat for 2-3 minutes. At same time, saute vegetables on medium heat until thoroughly heated yet crisp. Place loin cuts on French bread slices and cover meat with sauteed vegetables.

Mark Madison
Cambridge, New York

Hunter's Safety ...

When raising and lowering firearms to and from a tree stand, be sure that they are unloaded and have open actions.

Venison Fajitas

Serves: 3-4
Prep Time: 1 hour, 30 minutes

1	lb. venison steak, cut into thin strips
1	T. red wine vinegar
1	T. soy sauce
1	T. white wine
2	garlic cloves, crushed
2	T. olive oil
1/2	cup onions, diced
6-8	flour or corn tortillas
1/2	cup green peppers, diced
1/2	cup tomatoes, diced

Place venison slices in large bowl. Add vinegar, soy sauce, wine and 1 garlic clove; marinate for 1 hour. In skillet, put 1 T. olive oil and drained meat. Cook venison for about 5 minutes, stirring constantly until tender. Remove venison and add remaining olive oil, garlic and onions. Warm tortillas in oven or microwave. Put venison mixture, green peppers and tomatoes in tortillas. Serve with guacamole.

Stan Roesch
Harrisburg, Pennsylvania

Hunter's Safety ...

You should keep the action of the firearm open, except when actually shooting or when storing an unloaded gun.

My Favorite Venison Recipe

Recipe Name ——————————————

Serves ——————————————

Prep Time ——————————————

Ingredients

_____ _____
_____ _____
_____ _____
_____ _____
_____ _____
_____ _____
_____ _____
_____ _____
_____ _____

Directions

_____
_____
_____
_____
_____
_____
_____
_____
_____
_____
_____
_____

Passing On The Tradition

by Don Brown

Muscles throughout my body were taut and my nerves tingly as I peered cautiously from behind a rock outcropping at the most magnificent Dall ram I had ever seen in the wild. I had been sheep hunting in Alaska since 1983 with hope of someday finding an extraordinary ram. Now, some 350 yards away, such a trophy was nearly in range!

Turning to me, my son, Jerry, asked, "Dad, are you going to try for him from here?"

I thought about my choices. Do I try from this distance, knowing that the angle and the 20- to 30-knot crosswind would make for a most difficult shot, or should we get closer? I studied the long ridge we shared with the ram. It was actually a sharp-edged arete formed by glaciation aeons ago; a large saddle, or deep depression, separated us from the ram. To make matters worse the ram was looking in our direction, but was not yet alerted to danger. If alerted, he only had to walk in the opposite direction a few feet, and he would disappear down the backside of the steep ridge. I certainly didn't want to alert him.

My 12-year-old son and I had carefully planned this hunting trip for months. We were hunting southwest of Tok, Alaska, deep in the Alaska Range—the range in which Mt. McKinley is located—in heavily glaciated mountains and plateaus where sheep can live out their lives without ever seeing a human being. This country is not for the faint of heart.

As we packed and repacked for the hunt, I reflected upon the words of Stony Burk: "Hunting makes me a complete person. The outdoors gives me an emotional anchor, a solid reference point in the order of life." How true. This was an opportunity to teach my son my hunting philosophy. It was his first big-game hunt, and I wanted it to be right.

After arriving in Tok, we were flown in two Super Cubs into the mountains on August 5 for a self-guided 10-day hunt. Our pilots, Charlie and Ron Warbelow, were real happy when they saw we had packed light. Both of our packs weighed 108 pounds, and we brought only one rifle—a Remington Model 700 .300 Win. Mag. with a 3x9 Bausch-Lomb scope—for the two of us. I felt reasonably safe flying with Charlie and Ron; they are two of the best bush pilots in Alaska—always putting safety first.

When the wind died down, we took off. We planned to land in a high cirque bowl—a deep, steep-walled basin—at the headwaters of a small creek. With my topographical map in one hand and my camera in the other, I watched as we passed over a magnificent and unspoiled wilderness. Sheep dotted the ridges and the benches below us. Arriving at the cirque bowl located at the head of two sharp aretes, Charlie and Ron made several approaches to test the wind direction and velocity, as well as to inspect the landing site. After determining it was safe to land, they brought the planes in one at a time. Landing uphill inside of a bowl was a hair-raising experience for Jerry and me, but it seemed to be routine for the pilots. After unloading the gear and saying goodbye, Charlie and Ron took off downhill and flew back to Tok. We would see them again August 15.

Jerry was really excited. He grabbed some gear and headed quickly for a small patch of green tundra to start

setting up our little camp. An inch of snow remained on the ground from a previous storm. While this did not dampen our spirits, I did hope for better weather.

As the sun sank behind the mountains, we glassed the surrounding area for sheep. Just before dark, several small rams, ewes and lambs appeared out of nowhere, grazing on a high bench about 1,000 yards away. Darkness set in quickly while we watched the sheep through our spotting scope. The wind came up, and suddenly it was cold. It was time to get into our sleeping bags and dream about tomorrow's hunt.

It was cold and windy as I lit the little camp stove and prepared our breakfast of oatmeal and raisins. When the morning chores were finished, we donned white hunting clothes and went to find sheep.

Walking south in a zig-zag pattern along a shale slide, we reached a pinnacle where we could do some glassing. After three hours of slipping and sliding on an almost vertical shale and rock slide, we were able to set up our spotting scope. We spotted several Dall rams on the adjacent craggy, snow-covered mountains, but none appeared large enough.

Then, as so often happens in sheep hunting, the weather turned bad. Clouds rushed across the valley, pushed by a strong wind. Jerry and I stayed low to the ground and tried to make a shelter out of our packs and rain gear. Jerry was awed by the fact that we now were inside a cloud and couldn't see more than 15 feet in any direction. An hour or so later, the clouds lifted and the wind diminished. Although we were soaked and a little chilled, we still had high hopes for a successful hunt.

Seeing more sheep, we quickly set up the spotting scope again. There were seven rams. One looked to be an acceptable full-curl ram. Even though it was late, we embarked on a two-hour stalk that brought us within 250 yards of the sheep. The biggest ram's horns looked to be about 36 inches with no brooming. We marked the location on our map in case we wanted to come back on opening day. It was almost dark so we headed back to camp.

The next several days found the two of us walking many miles up and down mountains. We waded across glacial streams and climbed almost vertical shale slides;

occasionally we were caught in rock slides that carried us part way down the mountain. I worried that the wind would push Jerry off the precipices that we encountered, but this did not happen.

We glassed the whole area until our eyes hurt. We marked the locations of legal rams on our topo map. We saw one grizzly bear up close, and we photographed ermine, rock pika, squirrels and marmots. We even saw some eagles!

The night before the season opened, Jerry and I considered the possibilities marked on our topo map over cups of hot chocolate. We talked about the rams we had seen and their locations. Most of the good rams were right on top of the aretes in the most inhospitable real estate you could imagine. One exceptional ram was on the rim of a cirque wall. Jerry believed we could climb that wall if we were careful. I said the wall was nearly vertical, then reminded him of my bad right knee. It was starting to click again in the joint, and I was taking aspirin for the pain. Jerry persisted and I finally agreed. We decided to climb the cirque wall in hopes the ram was still there.

We were up early the next morning. It was still cold and windy. The tent's shifting caused me to think several times about going back to sleep, but the excitement was too much. We ate breakfast, packed food for two days, taped up our feet to protect them against blistering and began our quest.

By the time we reached the base of the shale slide on the cirque wall, there were sprinkles of rain. We put on our rain gear and started up. Jerry was in great shape and he moved out in front easily. However, 'ole Dad was scratching and clawing for every inch. The trick to climbing a steep slide is to lean into the mountain and take slow, deliberate steps while carefully watching where you plant your feet. After every eight or 10 steps, you should stop to breathe. Two hours later we were halfway up; we dug into the side of the slide and ate a snack. Breathing heavily but trying to show no pain, I asked, "Isn't this fun, Jerry?" "Yes", he replied with a laugh. He knew the mountain was whipping my 42-year-old body.

Soon after our snack-stop, we reached the most difficult part of the climb. Fifty yards of almost-vertical rock climbing. I enjoy rock climbing; however, it becomes a real challenge with a pack on your back. I am by no means a professional climber but the desire to take a good ram won out over common sense. So, up we went.

There comes a time during almost any sheep hunt when you want to quit and go home. This was such a time for me. Jerry was having little difficulty and was almost to the top. I, on the other hand, was sprawled against the rock wall with my kelty pack pulling at my back. I couldn't go up, and I couldn't go down. With the gentle rain and light wind, I slowly and carefully unstrapped my pack with one hand and lowered it slowly. I was able to hang it on a sharp rock. Without the pack throwing me off-balance, I was able to maneuver and find a new route. I wondered, however, why I didn't take my wife's advice and take up bowling.

Jerry and I had another snack when we reached the top. We then followed a narrow sheep trail that we found along the edge of the rugged cirque rim. I advised Jerry to be very careful—just a few inches away was a 1,000-foot drop!

We had walked about 100 yards when I whispered to Jerry to stop. Something up ahead didn't look quite right. In among the rocks on a craggy knoll was what appeared to be the top of a rounded sheep horn. We immediately dropped to our knees. Glassing with our binoculars, we verified that it was a ram's horn. We moved quickly to a better vantage point and set up the spotting scope. There were two rams lying there; the smaller one had a three-quarter curl and the other appeared to have a full curl. The bigger ram's head was down, and he appeared to be sleeping. The smaller one was watching us, but didn't seem alarmed.

The light rain stopped and the clouds began lifting. The wind, however, seemed to grow stronger. The large ram raised his head. Even without looking through the scope, I could tell he was huge. The excitement was contagious. Jerry was frantically getting the spotting scope turned up to 30 power. I could see the excitement in his eyes. Jerry was spellbound by the sight of the two rams. The large ram moved his head from side to side, showing off his massive, golden horns.

For a few brief moments, Jerry and I shared something very special—something that only hunting buddies in the field can understand. As we took turns looking at this incredible ram, we both knew that he was the king of the mountain. This regal Dall ram now was silhouetted against a blue sky. Looking at Jerry, I knew that he felt the same exhilaration. I will remember that moment forever. I was fulfilling a dream, and he was here to share my dream and have one of his own.

Leaving our packs, we began a slow stalk. We crawled on our hands and knees, reaching a spot where we could not move any closer or we'd spook the rams.

The large ram now was watching us carefully. This is why I believe in wearing white clothing; sheep seem less likely to run when they see white objects. I decided not to move closer, and would try an uphill shot at between 325

and 350 yards. This would be too difficult a shot for Jerry.

Jerry would watch through the binoculars for the bullet's impact, particularly if I missed. Considering the range and the wind, I felt there was a good chance of a miss. With his help, however, I might get off a good second shot before the ram disappeared.

Minutes seemed like hours when waiting for the ram to get uneasy and stand up to stretch. The wind seemed to die down as I laid the cross hairs just behind the ram's front shoulder and squeezed the trigger. The ram lurched and ran. Thinking I had missed, I asked, "Jerry, where did the bullet hit?" He replied, "I see blood, Dad." Just then, the ram fell and skidded a few feet. I knew it was over. The ram apparently died instantly. All of the squirrel hunting with a single-shot .22 rifle that I had done in Arkansas as a boy had paid off. It was a good shot. Feeling a warm glow come over me, I looked at Jerry who was grinning ear to ear. Neither of us noticed the cold, icy wind.

I told Jerry to go ahead on up to the ram; I would get the packs and be along shortly. I really wanted to be alone for a little while to savor the moment. I knew (even before seeing the ram up close) I had taken my greatest trophy in 30 years of hunting. I probably would never experience this kind of thrill again.

I picked up the packs and puffed my way to Jerry and

the ram. The Dall ram was everything I had imagined ... he was BIG! The magnificent animal lay only a few feet from the cliff's edge with a sheer drop of 800 to 900 feet.

Jerry and I pulled the sheep to a safer place. We took pictures and congratulated each other repeatedly. Then I measured the horns—the left was 42 inches and the right 40 inches; the bases were 14 inches. After the required 60-day drying period, the ram would score less. I didn't care because this was a truly great ram!

The trip down the mountain was difficult. Carrying a heavy pack and favoring my bad knee, I felt lucky to make it back to base camp without any serious problems. Jerry was a source of inspiration—I would love to have some of that athletic ability.

This trip was obviously a thrill of a lifetime for me. My son took a beautiful, full-curl, 36-inch ram in the same general area a few days later. Jerry also had experienced the thrills and excitement that hunting offers, as well as the close friendships made in the field.

Oh, I almost forgot ... Just before the Super Cubs came roaring in to pick us up, we saw a Dall ram high on a ridge framed against the blue sky, which, I swear, had 45-inch horns!

Other Big Game Recipes

Chili Margarita

Serves: 6-8
Prep Time: 4 hours

3	lbs. wild boar shoulder, cubed	2	jalepeno peppers, chopped (with seeds)
1	cup flour salt and pepper	1	green bell pepper, chopped
2	tsp. whole cumin seed	8	tomatillos, chopped
6	T. peanut oil	2	limes
1	jigger tequila	3	T. cilantro, chopped
3	large onions, chopped	1-2	beef bouillon cubes
1	12-oz. can beer water		
1	tsp. ground cumin		
1/2	tsp. sage		
1	bay leaf		
1	tsp. whole peppercorns		
4	ancho chilis (long, green)		

Combine flour and salt and pepper; coat meat cubes. Cook cumin seeds in heated peanut oil for 15 seconds. Add floured pork meat and saute until brown, stirring frequently; remove. Heat tequila until warm, then pour over meat. Using care, ignite tequila with match and allow flames to subside. Add onions to pan, using juices to stir browned bits. Cook for 8-10 minutes until soft. (Add more oil if necessary.) When onions are done, return meat to pan and add beer; stir. Add water to cover along with cumin, sage, bay leaf and peppercorns; simmer. Place ancho chilis under broiler and cook until skin blackens and blisters, turning often. Put chilis in paper bag (closed) for 5 minutes, then remove skin and seed and chop them. Add anchos, jalepenos, green bell pepper and tomatillos to chili. Squeeze lime juice into chili, add one lime to mix and discard the other. Bake at 325 degress for 3 hours. Remove lime and bay leaf. Stir in cilantro and bouillon cubes. Serve over rice.

Susan Good
Novato, California

Wild Boar Chili

Serves: 4-6
Prep Time: 1 hour

2   lbs. wild-boar meat, diced
6   tomatillas, diced
2   T. cooking oil
6   jalapeno chilis
2   tomatoes, sliced
1   small celery stalk, diced
3   large onions, diced
2   large cans chili or kidney beans
1   T. chili powder
    toppings, such as cheese or sour cream

Peel tomatilla outer shrouds and discard. In large Dutch oven, brown boar meat in oil. Add remaining ingredients. (Up to six more jalepeno chilis may be added to taste.)Add enough water to cover ingredients and simmer until tender, about 30-40 minutes. Add toppings when chili is served.

Charlie Valenta
Stickney, Illinois

Hunting Tip ...

Topographical maps are an invaluable aid in pre-season scouting. Mark the location of animals spotted during scouting on your map. They may still be in the area when hunting season arrives.

Whiskey-Fennel Sausage

Serves: 8
Prep Time: 1 hour

2	lbs. wild-boar shoulder, breast or hocks, cubed
6	oz. salt pork or bacon
2	bay leaves, finely crumbled
2	medium garlic cloves
1	tsp. ground coriander
1/2	tsp. dried red pepper flakes
1/2	tsp. sage
1/2	tsp. ground cumin
1/2	tsp. basil
1/2	tsp. marjoram
2	tsp. fennel seed
2	T. whiskey, scotch or bourbon
1	tsp. black pepper

Grind meat with all ingredients using mixer or food processor. (If using mixer or food processor, be careful not to grind sausage too fine.) Shape ground mixture into patties and grill for dinner or fry for breakfast.

Susan Good
Novato, California

Hunting Tip ...

Bowhunters need to be close. Forty yards should be the maximum range for most bowhunters, and 20 to 30 yards is better.

Whistle Pig Burgers

Serves: 8-10
Prep Time: 30 minutes

2   lbs. wild-boar meat, ground
1   lb. smoked ham
1   large onion, chopped
    salt and pepper to taste
    flour
    vegetable shortening
    soy sauce to taste

Combine meat, onion and salt and pepper; form patties. Dredge patties in flour and fry in shortening until brown. Serve with soy sauce.

Turk Tangert
Lancaster, Pennsylvania

Javelina Tagebrina

Serves: varies
Prep Time: 1 hour

1¹/2   lbs. javelina
1   8-oz. pkg. noodles
2   cups green pepper, diced
1   onion, diced
2   garlic cloves, diced
1   can creamed corn
1   can sliced mushrooms
1   cup tomato sauce
1   cup tomato juice
    cheddar cheese, grated

Prepare noodles while sauteing meat, green peppers, onion and garlic. Drain noodles; add corn, mushrooms, tomato sauce, juice and meat. Put grated cheese on top and bake in casserole for 40 minutes at 350 degrees.

Patrick Bingham
Tucson, Arizona

Zahino-Peccary

Serves: several
Prep Time: 2-3 hours

1 wild boar
1 garlic clove, slivered
1 tsp. salt
1 tsp. red pepper, crushed
1 tsp. black pepper
1 large onion, diced
   rum for basting
1 bottle beer
1 lime or orange

Remove musk gland from boar. Skin and split boar in half.
Insert garlic slivers into meat. Combine spices with onion
and enough rum to make a thin paste. Rub mixture over
meat. Barbecue over moderate fire. Baste with mixture of 1
bottle beer to juice of 1 lime or 1 orange.

S. J. Bellofatto
Columbus, Georgia

Hunter's Safety ...

*Beware of fatigue. When you become so tired that
hunting isn't fun anymore, go back to camp. Fatigue
can cause carelessness and clumsiness; it can also
make you see things that aren't really there.*

Javelina Chili

Serves: 6-8
Prep Time: 8-10 hours

2¹/₂	lbs. javelina	2	15-oz. cans kidney
1¹/₂	cups onion, chopped		beans
2	garlic cloves, diced	1	15-oz. can chopped
1	jalepeno pepper, diced		tomatoes
1	green pepper, sliced	1	T. cayenne pepper
	cooking oil	¹/₂	tsp. cumin

Saute meat, onion, garlic and peppers in cooking oil. Put in Crockpot, adding beans, tomatoes and seasonings. Cook on low setting for 8-10 hours.

Patrick Bingham
Tucson, Arizona

Andre's Wild-Game Burger By The Yard

Serves: 6-8
Prep Time: 45 minutes

2   lbs. ground big-game meat (any kind)
    mustard to taste
    catsup to taste
    relish to taste
    onions, diced
    tomatoes, diced
    your choice of seasonings to taste
1   loaf French bread
    cheese slices (any kind)

Combine mustard, catsup, relish, onions, tomatoes, seasonings and ground meat. Slice bread lengthwise, then into smaller pieces. Spread mixture onto bread pieces and bake at 350 degrees for about 20-30 minutes. Melt cheese slices on top of mixture during last few minutes of baking.

Charlie Valenta
Stickney, Illinois

Wild Summer Sausage

Serves: varies
Prep Time: overnight plus 3 hours

3	lbs. ground big-game meat (any kind)
1/2	tsp. salt
1/2	tsp. pepper
1	tsp. garlic powder
1	tsp. onion powder
2	T. Morton Tender Quick
1	T. liquid smoke
1	T. mustard seed
2	cracked peppercorns
3/4	cup water

Combine all ingredients, except meat, with water. Add solution to meat, mixing thoroughly. Refrigerate for 24 hours. Pack into sausage casings or roll into tube shape and wrap tightly with aluminum foil. (Poke holes in bottom of foil.) Bake for 3 hours at 250 degrees.

Joel Degel
Puyallup, Washington

Hunting Tip ...

If you need to approach a scrape, wear rubber boots and gloves; some hunters also wear a rubber rain suit. A few drops of deer urine on your boots and pants won't hurt, either.

Bill's Game Stew

Serves: 6
Prep Time: 6 hours

3	cups big-game meat, cut into bite-sized chunks
	salt and pepper to taste
	flour
	cooking oil
1	carrot, chopped
1	celery stalk, diced
1	onion, minced
1	potato, sliced
1	can stewed tomatoes
1	T. Worcestershire sauce
1	T. lemon juice
1	bay leaf
1	garlic clove, minced

Roll meat chunks in seasoned flour. Brown meat in hot oil. Place meat in Crockpot. Add remaining ingredients. Cook on low heat for 6 hours.

Bill Schmidt
Clovis, California

Hunter's Safety ...

Don't tie yourself in a tree stand with a rope. The rope could draw tight around your chest and leave you dangling. If you fall, fling your firearm or bow and broadheads as far away as possible.

Wild Breakfast Sausage

Serves: varies
Prep Time: 30 minutes

5	lbs. ground big-game meat (any kind)
1	lb. ground pork fat
1	T. salt
2	T. Morton Tender Quick
1/2	oz. garlic juice
1/3	cup water

Combine ground meat and fat. Mix remaining ingredients together; add to meat. Mix well. Grind mixture again.

Joe Degel
Puyallup, Washington

Bruce's Game Stew

Serves: 6-8
Prep Time: 5 hours, 30 minutes

2	lbs. big-game stew meat, cubed	3	tsp. tapioca
2	cups carrots, sliced	1	tsp. salt
2	cups potatoes, sliced	2	tsp. sugar
2	cups celery, diced	1/2	tsp. pepper
4	medium onions, sliced	1/2	cup water
2	cans stewed tomatoes	1	pkg. dry onion soup mix

Brown meat in large pot or skillet. Add remaining ingredients and slow-cook at 250 degrees for 5 hours. Add water to thin gravy, if needed.

Bruce Bitterman
Bismarck, North Dakota

Big-Game Cheeseburger Pie

Serves: 6
Prep Time: 1 hour, 30 minutes

2	lbs. ground big-game meat (any kind)		$1/4$	tsp. black pepper
$1/2$	cup onion, diced		2	cups flour
2	T. vegetable oil		1	tsp. salt
1	8-oz. can tomato sauce		$2/3$	cup shortening
1	4-oz. can mushrooms, drained and chopped			cold water
$1/4$	tsp. garlic salt		3	eggs
$1/4$	tsp. onion powder		6	cheddar cheese slices

In skillet, brown ground meat and onion in oil. Stir in tomato sauce, mushrooms, garlic salt, onion powder and black pepper. Simmer for 15-20 minutes.

Prepare pastry for double-crust pie: Mix flour and salt together in medium-sized bowl. Add shortening. Using a fork, cut in shortening until pieces are the size of small peas. Sprinkle 3 T. cold water over mixture and gently toss with fork, repeating until all flour is moistened. Form dough into 2 balls. Flatten one ball with hand and roll out on floured surface, forming a 12-inch circle. Ease pastry into 9-inch pie pan and trim even with pan's edge. Roll out remaining dough and retain for top crust.

Separate one egg and set yolk aside. Beat egg white with remaining eggs. Pour half of beaten egg mixture over bottom of pie shell. Spoon in meat mixture and arrange cheese slices on top; spread remaining beaten egg mixture over cheese. Mix 1 T. cold water with reserved egg yolk and lightly brush over edge of pastry. Reserve remaining yolk mixture. Add top crust, trimming dough $1/2$ inch over pie pan. Turn under bottom crust, seal and flute edge. Cut 4 slits in center of top crust and brush with reserved yolk mixture. Bake at 350 degrees for 40 minutes. Let stand for 10 minutes before serving.

Bradley Flategraff
Gallatin Gateway, Montana

Jerky—Raymond Style

Serves: varies
Prep Time: overnight plus 4-6 hours

	big-game meat (any kind)
2	cups burgundy or rose wine
1	T. non-iodized salt
3	T. soy sauce

Cut meat into 1/4-inch-thick strips. Combine meat with wine, salt and soy sauce to make marinade. Marinate meat strips for 24 hours in refrigerator. Drain strips of meat and smoke for 4-6 hours until done. Store in plastic bags and freeze.

Richard Raymond
Coeur d'Alene, Idaho

Bison Chili

Serves: 8
Prep Time: 1 hour, 30 minutes

3	lbs. ground bison meat	1	T. ground black pepper
	cooking oil	1	tsp. cayenne pepper
2	large onions, chopped	4	cups catsup
1	16-oz. can peeled	1	tsp. garlic
	tomatoes	2	tsp. cilantro
1	T. chili powder	1	tsp. thyme
1	25-oz. can kidney beans	1/2	tsp. powdered
1	25-oz. can chili beans		mustard

Fry meat in cooking oil; drain. In large pan or Crockpot, add cooked meat and remaining ingredients. Simmer for at least 1 hour. Serve with baked potatoes and grated cheese.

Thomas Hirsch
Madison, Wisconsin

Bison Stew

Serves: 6-8
Prep Time: 1 hour, 30 minutes

2	lbs. bison meat, cubed	2	tsp. salt
2	T. cooking oil	1/2	tsp. pepper
2	onions, chopped	3	medium potatoes,
2	2-oz. cans tomato sauce		peeled and sliced
6	carrots, peeled	1/2	cup water
	and sliced		
1	8-oz. can peeled		
	tomatoes		

In large kettle or Dutch oven, brown meat in oil. Add onions and cook until golden brown. Add tomato sauce, carrots, tomatoes and seasonings. Cover and cook for 1 hour on low heat. Add potatoes and water. Cover and cook another 30 minutes on low heat. Serve with lightly browned biscuits.

Thomas Hirsch
Madison, Wisconsin

Crockpot Bison Roast

Serves: 8-10
Prep Time: 8-12 hours

3-4	lbs. bison chuck roast (frozen)
	salt and pepper to taste
	salt to taste
	garlic and onion powder to taste
1/2	cup water

Place frozen roast in Crockpot. Add seasonings to water and pour over roast. Cook on lowest setting for 8-12 hours or until meat is tender. Slice and serve with drippings.

Thomas Hirsch
Madison, Wisconsin

Caribou Steaks

Serves: varies
Prep Time: 30 minutes

> caribou steaks
> 1 egg
> 1 cup flour
> 1 cup corn muffin mix
> 1/2 cup beer
> salt and pepper to taste
> water
> cooking oil

Cut meat into 1-inch-wide strips. Combine egg, flour, corn muffin mix, beer, salt and pepper and water. Dip each strip into corn muffin batter. Fry in cooking oil until golden brown on both sides.

Kerry Schoenborn
Molalla, Oregon

Hunting Tip ...

Searching for shed antlers and noting the location of those you find can give you valuable information about the size of deer and their haunts. This information will be helpful for next hunting season.

Caribou Hot Pot

Serves: 6
Prep Time: 3 hours

1-2	lbs. lean caribou meat, cubed
	potatoes, sliced 1/2 inch thick
	onions, sliced
3/4	tsp. salt
3/4	tsp. paprika
1	16-oz. can stewed tomatoes
1/3	cup sour cream or plain yogurt

In medium casserole, arrange meat, potatoes and onions in alternating layers. Combine salt, paprika and tomatoes; spread over layered meat and vegetables. Cover and bake at 350 degrees for 2 hours. Thirty minutes before casserole is done, stir in sour cream or yogurt.

John Snelling
Anchorage, Alaska

Hunter's Safety ...

Be sure of your target and beyond. Identify the target, then look past it to make sure it is safe to shoot. Do not shoot where your bullets might ricochet off rocks, trees, metal, water or other hard surfaces.

Other Big Game

Healthy Caribou Burgers

Serves: 4-6
Prep Time: 20 minutes

    2   lbs. ground caribou
   15   soda crackers
    5   tsp. dried onion
   1/2 tsp. garlic powder
    4   egg whites (discard yolks)
    2   T. steak sauce
        black pepper to taste

Crumble soda crackers and combine with other ingredients.
Shape mixture into patties. Fry patties in skillet until desired
doneness.

Bill Shipton
Las Cruces, New Mexico

Barbecued Moose

Serves: 8-10
Prep Time: 6 hours

    1   7-lb. moose roast
        salt and pepper to taste
    1   medium onion, sliced
    1   26-oz. bottle catsup
    1   qt. ginger ale

Place roast in roasting pan. Season roast with salt and pepper and spread sliced onion over top. Combine catsup and
ginger ale and spoon over and around roast. Roast for 6
hours at 325 degrees. Before serving, cut roast into thin
slices and return to sauce. Heat thoroughly and serve.

Bruce Bitterman
Bismarck, North Dakota

Moose Goulash

Serves: 3-4
Prep Time: varies

1   lb. moose stew meat
1   medium onion, diced
1   dash garlic
1   T. cooking oil
1   can tomato sauce
1/2 cup water
1   tsp. paprika
1   pinch basil
    salt and pepper to taste
1   red pepper, cubed
1   green pepper, cubed
1/2 cup sour cream

Saute meat, onion and garlic in oil. Add tomato sauce, water and seasonings. Bring to a boil. Reduce heat. Add red and green peppers and simmer for 10 minutes. Remove from heat and stir in sour cream. Serve over noodles.

Ty Duff
Sparks, Nevada

Hunting Tip ...

A bow with a draw weight of 50 pounds is considered the minimum for most big-game animals. When taking bear, for example, a bow weighing from 60 to 70 pounds would be the ideal minimum.

Moose Stew

Serves: 6-8
Prep Time: 2 hours

2	lbs. moose neck meat
1	medium onion, diced
1	tsp. garlic
2	T. cooking oil
2	cups water
1	cup burgundy
1/2	tsp. paprika
1/2	tsp. basil
	salt and pepper to taste
2	cups potatoes, diced
2	cups carrots, diced
1	cup celery, diced

In Dutch oven, brown meat with onion and garlic in oil. Add water, burgundy and seasonings. Cover and simmer for 1 hour. Add vegetables and simmer for another hour until tender.

Ty Duff
Sparks, Nevada

Hunter's Ethics ...

Realize that a hunting trip's success is not measured by how quickly you can take your limit. Strive to enjoy the hunt as a means of recreation; taking game should only be a small part.

Moose Stew With Dumplings

Serves: 4-6
Prep Time: 3 hours, 45 minutes

1¹/2   lbs. moose round steak, cut into 2-inch cubes
      flour
  4   T. cooking oil
  2   tsp. salt
      pepper to taste
2¹/2   cups water
6-8   carrots, peeled and sliced
6-8   potatoes, peeled and sliced
  4   onions
  2   cups dry biscuit mix
²/3   cup milk

Roll meat in flour and brown in oil. Add salt, pepper and water. Simmer on low heat for approximately 3 hours. Add vegetables and cook for 15 minutes. Combine biscuit mix and milk and drop by spoonfuls into stew. Cover and simmer for 12-15 minutes.

Joseph Thompson
Wiliamson, New York

Did You Know ...

Hunters who had purchased guns within a five-year period were analyzed, and the number who purchased handguns was the same as those that purchased either rifles or shotguns.

Moose Meat Loaf

Serves: 4-6
Prep Time: 1 hour, 30 minutes

1	lb. moose, ground
1/2	lb. pork, ground
1/2	cup onion, diced
2	T. parsley
1	egg, beaten
1/2	cup soda crackers, crumbled
1	cup tomato juice
	salt and pepper to taste

Mix all ingredients together and press into 9x5x3-inch loaf pan. Bake uncovered at 350 degree for 1 hour, 30 minutes.

Ty Duff
Sparks, Nevada

Did You Know ...

Waterfowl hunting members purchase the most factory-loaded ammunition, averaging 15.6 boxes a year per buying member. Upland bird hunters were next with an average of 14.4 boxes of shells. White-tailed deer hunters buy an average of 12.6 boxes.

Moosemeat Favorite

Serves: 6-8
Prep Time: 2 hours, 20 minutes

2	lbs. moose meat, cut into bite-sized pieces
2	T. cooking oil
1/2	pkg. dry onion soup mix
	water
1	can mushrooms
1/4	cup flour
1	T. basil
1	cup rice

Brown meat in oil. Add soup mix and enough water to cover meat. Simmer for 2 hours. Add mushrooms and thicken with flour and water. In separate pan, combine basil and rice and cook for 20 minutes. Serve meat mixture over rice.

Taj K. Uhde
Enumclaw, Washington

Hunting Tip ...

Scrapes are best observed from a distance so that you don't contaminate them with your scent. A buck usually revisits scrapes several times unless it is contaminated.

Healthy Moose Chili

Serves: 5-6
Prep Time: 1 hour, 30 minutes

20	oz. moose meat, cubed
1	T. canola oil
3	cups water
3	8-oz. cans tomato sauce
2	T. chili powder
1/2	tsp. ground cumin
1	cup onions, chopped
2	T. cornstarch
	mozzarella cheese, shredded

In iron skillet, brown meat in oil until tender. Add remaining ingredients, except cornstarch and cheese. Bring to a boil; thicken with cornstarch if needed. Sprinkle mozzarella cheese on top before serving.

Bill Shipton
Las Cruces, New Mexico

Hunting Tip ...

If you're hunting in a new area, don't be afraid to ask the local residents questions. You can get valuable information and prevent wasting valuable time in the field.

Zucchini Squash Stuffed With Moose

Serves: 4-6
Prep Time: 30 minutes

  2 lbs. moose meat, ground
  6 zucchini squash
 1/2 cup safflower oil
     salt and cayenne pepper to taste
  2 cups rice, cooked
  1 onion, chopped
  1 green pepper, chopped

Steam zucchini until tender. Scrape out centers and set aside; discard seeds. Crumble ground meat and brown in oil with salt and cayenne pepper. Remove meat from heat. In separate pan, combine rice, onion and green pepper. Mix thoroughly. Add zucchini centers to mixture. Stuff hollowed out zucchinis with mixture and bake at 325 degrees for 30 minutes.

Steve Sandberg
Chugiak, Alaska

Hunter's Ethics ...

Consider yourself an invited guest of the landowner, seeking his permission and conducting yourself properly. That way, you will most likely be welcome in the future.

Moose Steak in Mirepoix (Vegetable Flavoring)

Serves: 4-6
Prep Time: 1 hour, 30 minutes

2	lbs. moose steaks
1/2	cup carrots, diced
1/2	cup celery, diced
1/2	cup onion, cubed
1	garlic clove, minced
1	T. butter or margarine
1/4	bay leaf
1/2	cup burgundy wine
11/2	cups beef broth
	salt and pepper to taste
1/4	cup flour

Saute vegetables and garlic in melted butter until onion is
translucent. Add bay leaf, burgundy and broth. Simmer for
5 minutes; set aside. Trim fat from meat to prevent curling.
Season meat with salt and pepper and dredge in flour.

Melt some more butter and brown steak quickly on both
sides in large skillet. Add vegetable and broth mixture, cover
tightly and simmer over low heat until meat is tender,
about 1 hour, 30 minutes. Serve with vegetable mixture
spooned over each piece.

John Snelling
Anchorage, Alaska

Alaskan Meat Roll

Serves: 6
Prep Time: 5 hours, 30 minutes

    2   lbs. ground moose
    1   cup soft bread crumbs
    1/2 lb. bacon or ham, ground
    1   onion, chopped
        salt and pepper to taste
        dry bread crumbs

Combine everything, except dry bread crumbs, in large mixing bowl. Form mixture into large roll, about 10 inches long. Wrap roll in waxed paper, then in thin cotton cloth. Tie both ends of cloth tightly. Place roll in large pot of boiling water. Bring to a boil again and reduce heat. Let simmer for 3 hours, keeping water level constant. Allow roll to cool in water. Remove cloth and paper. Roll in dry bread crumbs and serve cold.

John Snelling
Anchorage, Alaska

Moose Ribs Barbecue Sauce

Serves: several
Prep Time: 2 days plus 30 minutes

	moose ribs	1	cup cider vinegar
1/4	cup dry mustard	1/4	cup water
1/2	tsp. cayenne pepper	1/4	cup real maple syrup
1	T. salt	1/2	cup butter

Mix seasonings together and combine with vinegar, water and syrup in saucepan. Bring to a boil, then add butter and cool. Apply sauce to ribs and refrigerate for 2 days. Barbecue and serve.

Steve Sandberg
Chugiak, Alaska

Bear Stew

Serves: 4
Prep Time: overnight plus 3 hours

	bear meat, cut into $1/4$-inch cubes
4	potatoes, sliced
3	carrots, sliced
2	large onions, diced
2	bell peppers, diced
1	T. cumin seeds
	salt and pepper to taste

Soak bear chunks in saltwater overnight. Rinse off next morning. Put bear meat in deep pan on low heat. Add vegetables and seasonings. Cover with water. Cook for 3 hours.

Gene Smith
Corning, California

Connie And Dave's Bear-Meat Supper

Serves: 6-8
Prep Time: 30 minutes

2	lbs. bear meat, diced
1	stick butter
5	large potatoes, sliced
1	medium onion, chopped
	salt and pepper to taste

Melt butter in skillet. Add potatoes and cook for 10 minutes. Add bear meat and onion. Cook for 20 minutes on medium heat. Season with salt and pepper.

Dave Coy
Hoyt Lakes, Minnesota

Potted Bear Meat

Serves: 8
Prep Time: 1 hour, 30 minutes

2	lbs. bear meat
3	large onions, chopped
3	T. shortening
3	T. flour
1	tsp. salt
1/4	tsp. pepper
1/4	tsp. thyme
1	pt. boiling water
2	T. vinegar
1	T. catsup

Cook onions slowly in shortening until brown. Cut bear meat into small pieces. Add meat to pan. Increase heat and brown meat on both sides. Combine flour with seasonings and sprinkle seasoned flour over meat. Add boiling water, vinegar and catsup. Cover and simmer until meat is tender, about 1 hour, 30 minutes.

Jack Barnes
Dallas, Texas

Hunter's Safety ...

Keep broadheads covered at all times when bowhunting, except when the arrow is actually nocked. Always be aware of people around you when you have a broadhead exposed.

Blue Cheese Stuffed Bear Steak

Serves: 4-6
Prep Time: 1 hour, 30-40 minutes

1	sirloin or round bear steak (thick)
$^1/_4$	cup green peppers, diced
$^1/_4$	cup onions, diced
$^1/_4$	cup mushrooms, diced
$^1/_4$	cup celery, diced
$^1/_4$	cup oysters or clams, diced
$^1/_4$	lb. butter
	blue cheese

To make stuffing, fry green peppers, onions, mushrooms, celery and oysters in butter until tender. Remove from heat. Slice a pocket in steak and stuff mixture evenly in it. Secure opening with toothpicks. Broil steak to taste (about 20-45 minutes). Crumble blue cheese on top of steak and broil until cheese melts.

Charlie Valenta
Stickney, Illinois

Elk Stew

Serves: 8
Prep Time: 3-4 hours

3-4	lbs. elk meat, cubed	4-6	potatoes, sliced
	water	8-10	carrots
2	beef bouillon cubes		
1	pkg. dry onion soup mix		
1	bay leaf		
	salt, pepper and		
	garlic powder to taste		

Put meat in large pot. Add remaining ingredients. Cover with water. Bring to a boil; reduce heat and simmer for 3-4 hours.

Leigh Dozier
Quartz Hill, California

Layered Elk Florentine

Serves: 3-4
Prep Time: 1 hour

1	lb. elk, ground
4	oz. medium cooked noodles
1	cup tomato sauce
1	T. sugar
1/2	tsp. salt
1/4	tsp. garlic salt
1/8	tsp. pepper
8	oz. cream cheese
3	T. milk
2	T. onion, chopped
1	10-oz. pkg. spinach
1/2	cup cheddar cheese, shredded

Brown elk meat and remove from heat. Stir in noodles, tomato sauce, sugar, salt, garlic salt and pepper. Combine cream cheese, milk, onion and spinach in small bowl. Spoon half of meat mixture and half of cream-cheese mixture into 2-qt. casserole. Top with remaining meat mixture.

Bake (covered) at 350 degrees for 40 minutes. Uncover and spread remaining cream-cheese mixture on top. Sprinkle cheddar cheese over cream-cheese mixture. Bake at 350 degrees (uncovered) for another 10 minutes.

Scott Nielsen
Elko, Nevada

Elk Sloppy Joes

Serves: 8-10
Prep Time: 30 minutes

3	lbs. elk meat, ground
1	large onion, diced
1^1/2	cups tomato juice
^{1}/2	cup catsup
^{1}/4	cup Worcestershire sauce
1	tsp. chili powder
1	tsp. cumin
1	tsp. curry
1	tsp. celery salt
1	tsp. paprika
1	tsp. prepared mustard
1	tsp. vinegar
	salt to taste
3	T. flour
3	T. brown sugar

Brown meat with onion. Add tomato juice, catsup, Worcestershire sauce, chili powder, cumin, curry, celery salt, paprika, prepared mustard, vinegar and salt. Thicken with flour. Add brown sugar and simmer for 30 minutes. Spoon onto burger buns and serve.

Scott Nielsen
Elko, Nevada

Hunting Tip ...

When tracking, particularly in snow, stay with one track unless another track is obviously fresh.

Swiss Elk Steak

Serves: 6-8
Prep Time: 1 hour, 30 minutes

2	lbs. round or chuck elk steak, cut into 1-inch pieces
1/2	cup sifted flour
2	tsp. salt
1/2	tsp. pepper
1/4	cup shortening
2	cups canned tomatoes (with liquid)
1/2	cup onions, chopped
1/4	tsp. paprika

Combine flour, salt and pepper. Pound steak using edge of knife then dredge in seasoned flour. Slowly brown steak in shortening. Combine tomatoes, onion and paprika; pour over steaks. Bring to a boil, reduce heat and simmer for 1 hour, 30 minutes.

Scott Nielsen
Elko, Nevada

Did You Know ...

A survey indicates that 61 percent of shotgun hunters use different guns for different game. The rest use one shotgun for all types of game.

Elk Stroganoff

Serves: 3-4
Prep Time: 1 hour, 30 minutes

1	lb. elk meat, cubed
2	T. flour
8	oz. sour cream
2	tsp. instant beef bouillon
1/2	cup water
1/4	tsp. pepper
2	T. margarine or butter
1 1/2	cups fresh mushrooms, sliced
1/2	cup onion, chopped
1	garlic clove, minced

Combine flour and sour cream. Stir in bouillon granules, water and pepper; set aside. In large skillet, cook half of meat in margarine over high heat, stirring occasionally until done. Remove from heat and add remaining meat, mushrooms, onion and garlic. Cook and stir until meat is done and onion is tender. Add sour cream mixture. Cook over medium heat, stirring constantly, until bubbly. Serve over noodles.

Anne Robinson
Frisco, Colorado

Hunter's Safety ...

Never climb a tree with a firearm, bow, sharp broadheads or even a bow quiver in your hand. You should always raise and lower them with a rope.

Elkburger Pie

Serves: 4-6
Prep Time: 40 minutes

1	lb. elk, ground
1/2	cup onion, chopped
1	8-oz. can tomato sauce
1	4-oz. can mushrooms, chopped
1/4	cup snipped parsley
1/4	tsp. salt
1/4	tsp. oregano
1/8	tsp. pepper
2	pkgs. crescent dinner rolls
3	eggs
6	cheese slices
1	T. water

Brown meat with onion. Stir in tomato sauce, mushrooms and seasonings. Place one package of rolls in greased pie pan, pressing edges together to form shell, separate 1 egg and set yolk aside. Beat remaining eggs and extra egg white and pour half over shell. Spoon in meat mixture. Arrange cheese slices on top. Spread remaining egg mixture on cheese slices.

Mix reserved egg yolk and water. Brush edge of shell. Open second package of rolls and roll out to make top crust. Place over pan and seal edges of bottom crust. Cut slits in top and brush with remaining egg yolk. Bake at 350 degrees for 20 minutes. Cover with aluminum foil and bake an additional 20 minutes.

Anne Robinson
Frisco, Colorado

Elk Loaf

Serves: 8-10
Prep Time: 1 hour, 15 minutes

4^1/$_2$	lbs. elk meat, ground	1	egg
1	cup milk	^{1}/$_8$	tsp. garlic powder
^{1}/$_4$	tsp. dried sage	1	small onion, chopped
^{1}/$_2$	tsp. salt	1	T. Worcestershire sauce
^{1}/$_2$	tsp. dried mustard	^{1}/$_2$	cup catsup (chili
^{1}/$_4$	tsp. pepper		or barbecue sauce)
^{1}/$_2$	cup dry bread crumbs		

Combine all ingredients together, except catsup. Spread mixture in loaf pan. Spoon catsup over top. Bake at 350 degrees for 1 hour or until done.

Anne Robinson
Frisco, Colorado

Elk B-Q

Serves: 4
Prep Time: overnight plus 30 minutes

4   elk steaks
1   red onion, diced
    salt and pepper to taste
    paprika
    parsley, chopped
2   green bell peppers, chopped
3   garlic cloves, minced
    red wine

Mix onion, salt and pepper, paprika, parsley, green peppers and garlic in bowl. Spread mixture over elk steaks in pan. Cover with red wine and marinate overnight. Grill and enjoy.

Scott Jones
Fresno, California

Healthy Burritos

Serves: 3-4
Prep Time: 30-45 minutes

1/2	lb. ground antelope meat
6	egg beaters
2	egg whites (discard yolks)
2	T. green-onion tops
2	T. dried onion flakes
4	oz. mozzarella cheese
6-8	flour tortillas

Combine meat, egg beaters, egg whites, onion tops and flakes in large cast-iron skillet. Cook for about 20 minutes or until done. Add cheese, stirring until slightly melted. Remove from heat. Warm tortillas; fill with meat mixture and roll. Serve with your favorite salsa.

Bill Shipton
Las Cruces, New Mexico

Hunting Tip ...

While stalking game, walk with your face into the wind. If there is only a slight breeze, wet your finger to help you determine its direction.

My Favorite Wild Game Recipe

Recipe Name ——————————————————

Serves ——————————————————

Prep Time ——————————————————

Ingredients

—————————————— ——————————————

—————————————— ——————————————

—————————————— ——————————————

—————————————— ——————————————

—————————————— ——————————————

—————————————— ——————————————

—————————————— ——————————————

—————————————— ——————————————

Directions

————————————————————————————

————————————————————————————

————————————————————————————

————————————————————————————

————————————————————————————

————————————————————————————

————————————————————————————

————————————————————————————

————————————————————————————

————————————————————————————

————————————————————————————

————————————————————————————

New Hunters, Added Rewards

by Louis Bignami

P assing skills on to others remains a basic and joyful part of our hunting heritage that ensures its continuation. While game and trespass laws limit harvest, tradition and ethics control behavior of hunters who have learned the "right stuff." Ethical hunters don't shoot doves off wires, ducks off the water or quail off the ground even though such activities are technically legal. Ethical hunters learn to shoot well and kill cleanly. Bird hunters use dogs to limit the number of lost gamebirds. Everything else stops in the search for wounded game.

Such hunters supported wildlife projects for decades before animal rights activists, who, it should be noted, seem to know little about either hunting or ethics, raised their voices. But ethical hunters aren't an abundant breed. Their development requires an investment of time, care and—yes—love. It seems vital that these caring hunters teach those who wish to hunt the skills and, most importantly, the proper behavior in the field.

I learned this several years ago when I visited one of

Idaho's better pheasant hunting co-ops. As is too often the case, rain dampened opening-day hopes. My grizzled English Setter, Wassie Bear, sulked in the car. In his dotage, he preferred warm days, birds that didn't run and, if it could be managed on sunny days, points in the shade.

Friends had already led eager dogs out onto rice checks to be in advantageous starting positions for the opening by the time I chased Wassie out of the car. He pointed immediately and I shot my opening-day brace of roosters. With the season 10 minutes old, I was done for the day. After a couple of his usual sloppy retrieves, Wassie didn't seem ready to settle down. Two minutes' work, considering the amount of dog food and vet costs invested, seemed like rather a short-changed situation to me, too. So I let him out of the car again and he meandered back to the bullrush-filled dish and eased on point. Meanwhile, my buddies made caustic remarks about "the slowest dog in the West."

Looking back, it seems possible the co-op had stocked a batch of birds; they didn't run like wild birds. With my limit cooling on top of my 4-wheel drive, I started walking toward Wassie's point to flush the bird. A car pulled up and stopped. A chubby teenager dressed in new camo clothing from head to toe jumped out of the car.

"Dog got a bird? Gotta Bird?" he blurted as his dad unfolded his lanky frame from behind the wheel.

"Looks like it. I've limited. Want it?"

"Can I, Dad?

"Just don't miss," his father snapped.

Great, I thought. Now I know the kid will miss.

The boy loaded his new Remington 870 and moved in. Wassie stood staunch until a big cock pheasant, voiding from one end and cackling from the other, fired out of the bullrushes. Three quick shots (too quick really) occurred and three misses resulted as the bird sailed out over the rice checks toward another hunter whose 20-gauge dropped the bird with one shot.

"You blankety-blank. I showed you how to shoot. Give me the blankety-blank gun and get back in the car. You're done for the day."

I bit my lip, remembering my promise to my wife not to punch out folks just because they are cruel and stupid.

Instead, I smiled at the boy who now huddled in the front seat of his dad's car, his moist eyes locked ahead. I whistled Wassie back in, loaded up my vehicle and left firmly determined to do something about this kind of situation.

There is a better way. You can use this proven method to start anyone hunting. It begins with the realization that hunting is more than simply grabbing a gun and going out in the field to try to shoot something. In the 10 or 12 years since this episode at the co-op, I've tried to teach youngsters, women and other men the joy of hunting. Of course, I've benefited somewhat because the people I've taught in years past are now easing my hunts with offers to beat up the hill, tote the deer or elk, help set up camp or chase chukkars into range. Some even have youngsters of their own now so I'm looking forward to starting on the second generation soon. Sure, it's a pain at times, but, overall, I would probably pay for the chance to recapture that one-time feeling of joy when taking your first bird or animal.

It's mostly about basics. You definitely need to teach gun skills; in most states, new hunters must pass a gun safety course in order to buy a license. More important, though, is that new hunters need to know how to hunt safely and productively in the field. They need to understand the working of dogs and the importance of hunting camps, as well as how to find and humanely dispatch wounded game. They also need to know how to field dress and preserve game and gamebirds. They need to learn not to criticize your pup or the marksmanship of a fellow hunter, and how to share the field, blind or stands so everyone gets a fair—and safe—chance. For future big-game hunters, tracking and backpacking skills should be added to this list.

Most of all, new hunters need to experience the joys of hunting that have nothing to do with the kill. Good dog work or effective duck calling, which both can result in a fine shot, offer a special joy. Then, there is the happy-sad mixture of appreciation and regret that older and, I hope, wiser hunters share when they successfully complete their hunt.

Developing this mix of skills and the right attitude takes time. Only after it is mastered does the joy—the real joy—of a fine stalk, a good call or some decent dog work become the hunter's special reward. To develop this special mixture, new hunters—like pups—should spend some time in the field before they pick up a gun. I taught my wife this way. She feared guns when we were first married. Over time, the realization that pheasants, quail and other gamebirds and game tasted better than chicken or beef created an interest in her for the field. Now, we share days in the blind, she looks forward to deer and elk hunting and we co-author fish and wildgame cookbooks.

As you begin your new-hunter project each fall, start by bringing them along on short, half-day trips so that boredom isn't a problem. Pick "bluebird" days when the foliage is bright and the air is brisk. Don't dump them in a duck blind where they can't see anything and don't force beginners out during cold, rain-drenched days that only

dedicated hunters, the brain damaged and, I suppose, steelhead fishermen really enjoy.

Discuss your plans for tracking and the hunt on the way so they know what to expect. Teach youngsters the use of quail calls, but leave goose and duck call practice until it can be done outside.

Share information on plants and animals that you see. If you shoot something, dispatch it humanely before you call your new partner in for a look. Be willing to head back if the new hunter looks tired. If you hunt with dogs, invite the new hunter to take part in a training session and stress the importance of solid points and good retrieves.

Only after two or three such trips should the new hunter bring a gun to the field, and then only after he or she seems comfortable handling a weapon on a range. (I must admit to a prejudice that shotguns and bird hunting should come before rifles and big-game hunting.) I like to start new hunters in the spring or summer so they have more time in which to master gun-handling skills. Those who want to hunt ducks, for example, can invest some time watching duck-identification videos while other hunters might want to watch some of the better hunting videos.

Shotgunners can shoot at clay targets or spend $40 for a Daisy "Quick Skill" air rifle to practice shooting at still and moving targets at home. I try to teach two or three youngsters to shoot each year; I find most can learn to shoot well in a month or two. Bob Brister, in his excellent book on shotgunning, details a practice method in which you can shoot 1,500 BBs for less than the cost of a box of shotgun shells. With practice in shooting the air rifle, a shooter can learn to hit tossed quarters, and it's easy to make corrections because the shooter can follow the BB's flight. Don't start beginning bird hunters with a .410; the .410 is really an expert gun. Instead, try a 20-gauge or some tame handloads for a 12-gauge.

Rifle hunters also find it advantageous to practice with air rifles at home when the weather doesn't allow practicing at an outdoor range. Practicing in three positions at still and, then, moving targets ensures better results when you get to the field. For potential big-game hunters, the transition to .22 rifles and then to a gun with a mild recoil such as a .243 or .257 Roberts makes good sense.

Because safety comes first, the new hunter should attend any state-mandated classes. These classes help build that "nobody ever got in trouble passing on a shot" attitude that we all prefer. Then, invite your new hunter along on an empty-gun trip or two if you have the time. In this way, you can fine-tune gun safety procedures without risk. I also let youngsters bring their BB guns on several trips before they graduate to shotguns. This all helps.

Only after taking these basic steps should you try a day in the field. If you can, plan that initial outing at a pheasant preserve where lengthy seasons allow more time for training and big, slow birds raised for harvesting increase the novice's chances of a clean hit. When my wife, Annette, was learning to hunt, she shot her first two pheasants on a preserve. At many such preserves, $60 buys the beginner as many shots as is needed to harvest two large birds. Savvy preserves also include the use of a dog and an attendant to assist the hunter (they also generally make a fuss over first-time hunters).

The preserve-environment takes the pressure off new hunters. A missed bird won't fly far, and there are plenty of birds. You don't have to differentiate between hens and roosters because you can shoot both. And, if you like, the staff will clean the birds and prepare them for cooking or freezing.

You also can start new hunters on private property during the regular hunting season. Take the new hunter along when you seek permission to hunt; property owners who turn down most hunters find it difficult to refuse a first-time hunter. If you must start a new hunter on public property, select a weekday. There is simply too much confusion on weekends and opening day for beginners.

Preparation for that first hunt is important. If possible, have the new hunter shoot a few targets that morning or the evening before to help settle down. If you're starting with deer, be sure your rifles are sighted in properly. This is a good habit to instill in the new hunter. It emphasizes taking only those shots that will most likely result in a clean kill.

Remember, too, that there's a lot more to the joy of hunting than just the hunt. My wife, for example, insists on her special biscuits-and-gravy breakfast before deer hunts, but claims "wild rice pancakes go better with bird trips." Try to make the trip a ritual you will repeat from year to year. Cook a special breakfast or stop at a particular spot. Give yourself plenty of time to get into position— new hunters tend to rush.

Help your new hunter concentrate on the fun of the hunt rather than its results; savor with him or her the wonderful, one-time experience of taking the first bird. Above all else, put no pressure at all on the beginner; nobody hits every bird. Real altruists even miss a bird or two once in a while to show beginners that it's okay. When your new partner bags that first bird, send the pup out to fetch it or get it yourself. Take time to admire it while stressing that the bird's life was taken with respect and regard to conservation practices.

Wild Fowl Recipes

Microwave Quail Parmesan

Serves: 6-8
Prep Time: 30 minutes

6-8 quail
5 T. butter
2 T. flour
3/4 cup light cream
   Parmesan cheese
3 egg yolks, beaten
1/2 cup bread crumbs

In skillet, melt half of butter and brown quail. In saucepan, heat cream until boiling. In microwave pan, melt remaining butter. Add flour and blend. Add cream to flour and butter, mixing thoroughly. Add 1 T. cheese and stir in egg yolks. Sprinkle 1/4 cup cheese on bottom of separate glass baking dish. Put quail in dish and spoon sauce and bread crumbs over it. Cook in microwave for 14-16 minutes at 60 percent power.

Dean Hendrickson
Quartz Hill, California

Hunter's Ethics ...

Support conservation efforts that help ensure good hunting for future generations of America. Always give back to nature what it gives to you.

Butterflied Quail

Serves: 1-2
Prep Time: 1 hour, 30 minutes

1   quail
    butter
1   lemon
    white wine
    bread crumbs

Break quail breastbone to flatten using a heavy object, such as bread board, to flatten. Marinate quail in butter, lemon and white wine for at least 1 hour. Slowly broil bird on each side. Sprinkle bread crumbs over bird during last 2 minutes of cooking time.

Nancy Johnson
Mesa, Arizona

Quail Roasted With Ham

Serves: several
Prep Time: 1 hour

1   quail
    corned ham slices
    butter
    water

Clean quail and stuff with your favorite dressing. Place thin corned ham slices on quail. Then cover entire quail with white sheets of paper, securing with pack thread. Stitch papers together. Baste quail with butter and water. Roast for about 45 minutes. Remove papers and brown slightly before serving.

Tommy Parker
Edward, North Carolina

Spiced Butter Grouse

Serves: 2-3
Prep Time: 12-24 hours

2 fresh grouse breasts, halved
$^1/_2$ cup olive oil
$^1/_2$ tsp. ground hot pepper
$^1/_2$ tsp. garlic
$^1/_2$ tsp. salt
$^1/_2$ tsp. oregano
1 T. onion, ground
$^1/_2$ cup butter

Combine olive oil and dry ingredients. Place halved breasts in glass bowl and pour spiced oil on top. Mix breasts and oil until breasts are fully covered. Marinate in refrigerator for 12-24 hours. Drain breasts and fry in deep butter.

J. Noble Snowdeal
Bangor, Maine

Baked Grouse—Buffalo Style

Serves: 1-2
Prep Time: 2-3 hours

2 grouse
dressing or stuffing of your choice
2 hickory or smoked bacon strips

Skin and clean grouse. Stuff birds with dressing and lay bacon strips across breast of grouse. Wrap bird loosely in aluminum foil. Place in roasting pan and bake for 80-90 minutes at 350 degrees. Open foil. If fat from bacon has cooked into breast, uncover bird and bake for another 15-20 minutes.

James Deperto
Buffalo, New York

Roast Grouse

Serves: 1-2
Prep Time: 1 hour

> 2   grouse
> chicken-flavored rice
> water
> salt and pepper
> butter

Cook rice and set aside. Remove skin from grouse and wash thoroughly. Season birds with salt and pepper, then stuff with rice. Place birds in roasting pan. Add $^1/_2$ cup water. Saturate with butter. Cook covered at 350 degrees for 45 minutes, basting frequently with butter from the pan. Remove cover and cook until golden brown.

Kerry Schoenborn
Molalla, Oregon

Did You Know ...

About one in three hunters takes part in shooting sporting clays, a rapidly developing target shooting sport. Slightly more than 40 percent of hunters surveyed will find time to shoot with target rifles, pistols or shotguns.

Pheasant

Serves: 2-3
Prep Time: 15 minutes

1 pheasant
  salt and pepper to taste
3 T. butter
1/8 cup water
1 pt. thick cream
3 T. sherry

Season pheasant with salt and pepper. In saucepan, lightly brown bird in butter. Place pheasant in pressure cooker with water and cook at 15-lbs. pressure for 15 minutes or until tender. Remove bird from pressure cooker and place in large pan or skillet; cover with cream. Add sherry and simmer until cream is thick. Serve with wild rice.

Victor Lenegar
Wellston, Ohio

Did You Know ...

Most of the hunting basics (binoculars, camo gear, calls, boots and knives) will be found in virtually every NAHC Member's home. Airguns will be found in 42 percent of homes, tree stands in 40 percent and wildlife prints in 36.

Baked Pheasant In Sour Cream

Serves: 2-3
Prep Time: 1 hour, 30 minutes

1   pheasant
    salt and pepper
1   garlic clove, crushed
1$^{1}/_{2}$ T. butter or margarine, melted
1   pt. sour cream

Rub pheasant with salt, pepper and garlic. Brush with butter. Bake uncovered at 350 degrees until brown. Pour sour cream over bird and bake at 325 degrees until tender.

Lawrence Benson
Oil City, Pennsylvania

Braised Pheasant With Mushrooms

Serves: 6-8
Prep Time: 1 hour

2   pheasants, cut into serving-sized pieces
$^{1}/_{2}$ cup dry pancake mix
$^{1}/_{2}$ cup butter
2   cups sliced mushrooms
1   small onion, chopped
2   chicken bouillon cubes
    juice from $^{1}/_{2}$ lemon
1   tsp. salt
1   tsp. pepper

Dip pheasant pieces in pancake mix. Saute meat in butter until brown. Remove from skillet. Place mushrooms and onions in butter, sauteing until brown. Add pheasant, bouillon dissolved in hot water, lemon juice and seasonings. Cover and simmer for 1 hour or until tender.

Charles Weipert
Waterville, Iowa

One-Pot Pheasant Meal

Serves: 4
Prep Time: 1 hour, 30 minutes

  2   pheasants, cut into serving-sized pieces
4-6 juniper berries
  1   tsp. Herb de Provence
  1   onion, quartered
  1   green pepper, quartered
  1   can cream of mushroom soup
  1   can water
      garlic, salt and pepper to taste

Put pheasant pieces in cooking dish. Mix in other ingredients. (Be sure there is plenty of liquid.) Cook for 1 hour, 30 minutes at 350 degrees. Potatoes and carrots may be added if desired.

Leigh Dozier
Quartz Hill, California

Pheasant Cutlets

Serves: varies
Prep Time: 30-45 minutes

  1   pheasant, meat only
2-3 eggs, beaten
      Italian bread crumbs
      olive oil

Cut pheasant meat into 3-inch pieces and pound flat with tenderizing meat mallet. Dip meat into eggs and coat with Italian bread crumbs. Fry over low heat in olive oil until brown.

Norman Bernier
Newington, Connecticut

Sweet And Sour Pheasant

Serves: 3-4
Prep Time: 1 hour, 30 minutes

1	pheasant, boned and cut into cubes
2	T. vegetable oil
1	cup water
1	16-oz. can pineapple chunks
3	T. cornstarch
1/4	cup white vinegar
1/4	cup brown sugar
5-6	T. soy sauce
1/4	cup green pepper, chopped
3	T. onions, chopped

Brown pheasant cubes in oil. Cover with water and simmer for 1 hour; drain liquid. Drain pineapple, reserving juice. Combine pineapple juice, cornstarch, vinegar, brown sugar and soy sauce; add to meat and cook over medium heat until mixture becomes thick. Add green pepper, onion and pineapple. Heat thoroughly and serve with rice.

Dan Sowieja
Milwaukee, Wisconsin

Hunting Tip ...

Late-season ringneck pheasants are difficult to hunt. Look for them in the densest available cover, and they will most likely sit tight. A dog is invaluable for this type of hunting.

Doves Smothered In Gravy

Serves: 4-5
Prep Time: 2 hours

8-10	doves
6	T. flour
	salt and pepper to taste
1/4	tsp. ginger
3/4	cup olive oil
3	garlic cloves
1 1/2	cups red wine

Combine flour, salt and pepper and ginger. Wet doves and coat with flour mixture. Heat oil with garlic cloves and brown doves. Add wine and water; cover and simmer until tender (1 1/2-2 hours). Add leftover flour mixture to thicken gravy. Serve with rice.

David Harper
Huntsville, Alabama

Hunter's Ethics ...

Treat the game your hunting with extreme respect. Realize it is your responsibility to retrieve all downed game, regardless of the amount of time it takes.

Dove And Rice Casserole

Serves: 4
Prep Time: 1 hour, 30 minutes

8   doves
1   can cream of mushroom soup
1   can water
1/4 cup onion, minced
1/2 cup wild rice, cooked
1/2 cup white rice, cooked
2   T. butter or margarine
1   tsp. sage
     paprika

Combine soup and water. Mix all ingredients except paprika. Pour into 9x13-inch casserole. Press birds, breast-side up into mixture. Cover with aluminum foil and bake for 1 hour at 350 degrees. Uncover and baste birds with butter. Sprinkle paprika over birds and bake for 30 more minutes.

Dodman Nobel
Fortville, Indiana

Hunting Tip ...

No matter how quietly you to try to move, you'll make some noise. Try to imitate the noise that an animal would make when moving through cover.

Dove BBQ

Serves: varies
Prep Time: 1 hour, 30 minutes

dove breasts
butter or oil
wine (your choice)
$^1/_2$ tsp. garlic powder
$^1/_2$ tsp. seasoning salt
$^1/_2$ tsp. parsley

Marinate dove breasts in butter (or oil) and wine of equal amounts for at least 1 hour. Add seasonings; drain. Barbecue meat in basket for 20-30 minutes, basting with drained marinade during last 10 minutes.

Nancy Johnson
Mesa, Arizona

Drunken-Spicy Dove

Serves: varies
Prep Time: 1 hour, 30 minutes

dove breasts or parts
cooking wine (your choice)
$^1/_2$ cup jalapeno juice
garlic, chopped
jalapeno peppers to taste
red onion to taste
celery salt to taste
black pepper to taste

Spread dove breasts in saucepan. Pour in cooking wine to depth of $^1/_4$-$^1/_2$ inch. Add remaining ingredients and marinate for 1 hour. Cook over low heat, stirring frequently. (Meat is done when it peels easily.)

Scott Jones
Fresno, California

Buttered Doves

Serves: varies
Prep Time: 30 minutes

dove breasts
melted butter
lemon juice to taste
dill seed

Place dove breasts in deep glass or pottery baking dish;
cover with melted butter. Add lemon juice and dill seed.
Broil in oven for 15-20 minutes.

T. Sulmeisters
Conifer, Colorado

Barbecued Turkey

Serves: 6-8
Prep Time: 1 hour

1 turkey, cut into serving-sized pieces
1/2 cup green onion or chives, chopped
butter
garlic juice or garlic salt
1/4 cup lemon juice
1 T. thyme and savory, mixed
1 cup broth
3 T. parsley

Cook onions in butter until tender. Add remaining ingredients (except turkey) and bring to full boil. Immerse turkey
pieces in this mixture. Remove and cook on grill for 45 minutes or until done, basting often.

Daniel House
St. Charles, Missouri

Turkey Chow Mein

Serves: 3-4
Prep Time: 1 hour

1	lb. turkey, cut into serving-sized pieces
1	pkg. oriental seasoning mix
2	T. soy sauce
2	tsp. sugar
3/4	cup water
2	T. oil
2	celery stalks, finely sliced
1	green pepper, chopped
1	red pepper, chopped
1/4	lb. snow peas
1	onion, thinly sliced
2	cups bean sprouts

Combine seasoning mix, soy sauce, sugar and water. Mix and set aside. Heat oil in skillet. Add turkey and stir-fry, stirring constantly. Add celery when meat is cooked. Add remaining ingredients every 2 minutes in order: green pepper, red pepper, peas, onion and bean sprouts. Continue to stir constantly. After all ingredients are added, pour in mix and simmer for 2-5 minutes. Serve over rice.

Mike Neilson
Danville, Indiana

Did You Know ...

Two out of three hunters purchase new shotguns and rifles instead of buying used guns.

Camper's Covered-Skillet Turkey

Serves: 6-8
Prep Time: 1 hour

1	turkey, cut into serving-sized pieces
	butter or margarine
1	cup onions, chopped
1	cup mushrooms
1	cup parsley
	pepper to taste
1	can beer

Fry turkey pieces in butter or margarine; drain excess fat. Add remaining ingredients. Cook for 45-60 minutes on low heat.

Daniel House
St. Charles, Missouri

Wild-Turkey Breast

Serves: 3-4
Prep Time: 8 hours

1	turkey breast
4	T. butter
1	small, sweet onion
	dash of thyme, basil, mint, parsley
	salt and pepper to taste
1/2	cup apple juice

Put turkey in Crockpot and add butter. Sprinkle dry ingredients on top, then add apple juice. Cook on high setting for 8 hours.

Phillip Frame
Sutton, West Virginia

Easy Wild-Turkey Dinner

Serves: 3-4
Prep Time: 3-4 hours

1 wild turkey, skinned
1 stick margarine
4 carrots, skinned and halved
4 potatoes, peeled and sliced
1 pkg. bacon

Press margarine inside cavity along back of bird. Put carrots and potatoes inside cavity. Place turkey in roasting pan with enough water to enter cavity. Place bacon over breast of turkey. (You may need toothpicks to hold bacon in place.) Bake at 400 degrees, basting frequently, until tender and no blood appears. (Check water level often.) Broth makes excellent dressing and gravy.

Bill Hardee
Norfolk, Virginia

Hunter's Safety ...

Be sure your portable platform is securely chained or strapped to the tree. Check the platform itself for loose bolts or screws each time you use it.

Wild-Turkey Louis

Serves: 4
Prep Time: 45 minutes

1	lb. turkey breast, cut into cubes
2	T. margarine
1/4	cup green onion, sliced
1/4	tsp. salt
1/4	tsp. black pepper
3	T. flour
1	cup chicken broth
1/2	cup dry sherry
1/4	cup stuffed green olives, sliced
1	cup fresh mushrooms, sliced
1/2	tsp. dried tarragon

Heat margarine in skillet over medium heat. Quickly brown turkey cubes on all sides. Place turkey in 1-qt. casserole. Add onion, salt, pepper and flour to reserved drippings in skillet. Cook and stir for about a minute.

Remove pan from heat and slowly add broth and sherry. Stir until smooth. Return to heat and cook, stirring constantly, until mixture thickens. Add olives, mushrooms and tarragon, mixing thoroughly. Pour mixture over turkey. Cover and bake for 20-25 minutes at 350 degrees until tender.

John Judd
Mason, Michigan

New Jersey Chili

Serves: 2-4
Prep Time: 1 hour, 30 minutes

2   lbs. ground wild turkey
1   large onion, chopped
1   large green pepper, chopped
2   16-oz. cans kidney beans
2   chili peppers, chopped
2   T. chili powder
1   T. garlic powder
1   tsp. white vinegar
1   16-oz. can tomato sauce

Brown turkey meat in skillet. When meat is half-cooked, add onion and green pepper. When done, drain and put in soup pot. Add kidney beans, chili peppers, spices and vinegar. Stir in tomato sauce until desired thickness. Cook on low heat for at least 1 hour.

Joseph DiGiampaolo
Raritan, New Jersey

Hunting Tip ...

Shoot only if you can see the animal clearly enough to identify it. Don't shoot at moving branches without being able to see the animal behind them.

Crockpot Duck

Serves: 3-5
Prep Time: overnight plus 4 hours

3   ducks
    water
2   chicken-flavored bouillon cubes
    flour
    cooking oil
    salt and pepper to taste
1   5-oz. pkg. wild rice

Remove meat from bones. Place meat in bowl and cover
with cold water. Add bouillon cubes, cover and marinate
overnight. Dip meat in flour and fry in cooking oil. Season
meat with salt and pepper and fry until browned. Cook rice
as directed. When fully cooked, put thin layer of rice in bottom of Crockpot. Add layer of fried duck. Keep alternating
until both are gone. Then add 1/2 cup cold water. Cook on
high setting for 1 hour. Reduce heat to low setting and cook
for 3 hours or until meat is tender.

Rodger Nelson
Canton, Illinois

Hunting Tip ...

*When hunting turkeys, don't be afraid to change
calls or locations. Either change may be the required
action that will encourage reluctant gobblers to
move into range.*

Sweet And Sour Duck

Serves: 4-6
Prep Time: 1 hour, 15 minutes

5	lbs. duck meat pieces
2	T. butter or fat
2	cups sauerkraut
1	6-oz. can frozen orange juice
1/4	cup water
1/2	tsp. caraway seed

Melt butter or fat in large, heavy skillet. Add duck pieces and brown. Top with sauerkraut. Combine orange juice, water and caraway seeds; pour over sauerkraut. Cover and simmer for 1 hour, 15 minutes or until duck is tender.

Charles Weipert
Waterville, Iowa

Sauerbraten Goose

Serves: 1-2
Prep Time: 30 minutes

1/2	goose breast sauerbraten mix
1 1/2	cups water
2	T. sour cream

Brown goose breast in pressure cooker. Add sauerbraten mix and water. Seal pressure cooker and cook for 20-25 minutes. Add sour cream before serving, mixing well into gravy. For thicker sauce, use cornstarch. Slice and serve.

Raymond Bussnick
Emerson, New Jersey

Goose Pot Pie

Serves: 3-4
Prep Time: 2 hours

1   whole Canada goose breast, diced
1   chicken bouillon cube
    cornstarch or flour
5   medium potatoes, cooked and cubed
1/2 cup frozen peas
5   large carrots, cooked and sliced
1   batch biscuit dough

Boil goose with bouillon, saving about 4 cups broth. Thicken broth with cornstarch or flour to make smooth gravy. Add vegetables and goose to gravy. Pour entire mixture into shallow casserole. Cover goose and vegetables with dough and bake until biscuits are done.

J. Noble Snowdeal
Bangor, Maine

Orange Rice Dressing For Waterfowl

Serves: varies
Prep Time: 30 minutes

1   cup uncooked white rice (not instant!)
1/2 cup water
1/2 cup orange juice
1   garlic clove, chopped or pressed
1   T. dried parsley, chopped
1   tsp. Tabasco sauce

Combine all ingredients in 2-qt. covered pot and bring to boil. (Do not uncover pot during cooking time.) Turn heat to low and cook for 10 minutes. Remove from heat and let stand for 10 minutes. Fluff with fork and serve hot.

J. B. Willoughby
Bedford, Indiana

Waterfowl Soup

Serves: varies
Prep Time: 1 hour, 15 minutes

1 duck carcass
   chicken broth
   your favorite seasonings
   whole-wheat noodles or rice

Boil duck carcass for approximately 30 minutes until meat is soft enough to fall off bones. Remove meat and bones from broth and cool. Then, separate meat from bones, discarding bones. Trim any larger pieces. Add chicken broth, seasonings and noodles or rice. Simmer gently for about 30 minutes. Serve with crackers.

James Deperto
Buffalo, New York

Hunting Tip

When hunting geese, you don't always need to call them into your set—especially if flocks are circling. Remember that a bad call is worse than no call.

My Favorite Wild Fowl Recipe

Recipe Name ———————————————
Serves ———————————————
Prep Time ———————————————

Ingredients

——————————— ———————————
——————————— ———————————
——————————— ———————————
——————————— ———————————
——————————— ———————————
——————————— ———————————
——————————— ———————————
——————————— ———————————

Directions

————————————————————
————————————————————
————————————————————
————————————————————
————————————————————
————————————————————
————————————————————
————————————————————
————————————————————
————————————————————
————————————————————
————————————————————

Memories Are Made Of This

by Wayne Martin

With my heart pounding, I could feel my throat go dry when I saw the fresh-looking scrape in the semi-darkness while approaching my tree stand in the old, long-dead birch tree on Lake Francois. Maybe my calls late last night really had attracted a bull! This is a fresh scrape, and I am convinced that calling from a scrape area is much more effective than calling blind. The bull expects a cow to be at his scrape; when he hears the call, he comes in without hesitation.

Lance, my hunting partner, and I left home shortly before noon Sunday and stayed that night with our Canadian friends, Jacques and Mary, in Maniwaki, Quebec. We outfitted with Poirier Hunting and Fishing Territory like we have for many years. Having first hunted moose in Canada in 1969 and nearly every year thereafter, I look forward to each trip with almost the same excitement as the first. The four-hour trip from Maniwaki to the base camp included traveling 25 miles of dirt road and a 10-mile run by boat on the lake. You could say we are rather isolated for the week; we wouldn't have it any other way.

(Most of this story is taken from my hunting journal. I often make entries in it while I sit in my tree stand.) We set up our stands on Lake Francois (once called Hourglass lake because of its shape) where I killed my first moose with a bow, and where my cousin killed a Pope and Young bull in 1982.

On this, our first actual hunting day, a morning breeze drifted and the clouds still covered the sun. Even though the weather is warm, the wind cut right through me, forcing me to wear my jacket. I don't like wearing additional clothing because it's difficult to draw my bow. But today I was glad to have the jacket as I hunkered into the wind. After another hour of sitting in the wind, Lance and I went back to camp for lunch.

On the way, we saw several piles of bear scat. If the size of the pile is indicative of the size of the bear, the bear is huge! Some small, berry-bearing shrubs also were bent down across the trail, indicating that the bear had foraged recently. Close to camp, a spruce tree showed signs of clawing about 8 feet above the ground, indicating a bear had "marked" the tree. Within sight of the cabin, in fact, more of those berry shrubs were bent over. We hadn't even brought a backup firearm this time!

By the time we reached the cabin, the sun had come out and there was still a breeze, although a more pleasant one. Only a few clouds remained in the sky, perhaps reflecting a change in the weather. That plus our sighting yesterday of two full rainbows gave us hope that we were in for a good hunt.

We were back at our stands by 1 o'clock. I rested and called for most of the afternoon. Disgusted, I left my stand and talked with Lance about doing something different. We decided to reconnoiter Lake Claire, about a one-mile walk through the woods. We soon found fresh tracks along the trail. Perhaps it was a moose coming to my call. Oh well, it's too late now! The canoe was stashed at the end of the trail beside the beaver dam so we walked through the brush to the point on Lake Claire. Standing under a giant white pine, I called again. There was no wind and the air was comfortably warm. I napped while lying in the thick duff, awakening once in awhile so I could glass the far shore and make another call. Finally, at 6:40 p.m., I heard Lance's whistled call of the white-throated sparrow, our signal to move. I lost my way going back, but, fortunately, I recognized my back trail when I ran across it. It was getting dark as we paddled across Lake Francois and it was dark by the time we got to the cabin. By 9:30 we were sound asleep. Sleeping here is so easy and pleasant. All my worldly concerns are so far away; they just recede and are temporarily forgotten.

A little before 8 a.m. Wednesday, I heard it—the grunt of a bull moose. It was Lance's turn to call. Because this is the first response we have had, he gets credit for calling the first moose. I smiled and got ready. This moose would come down from the mountain, cross over the point and reach shore either near Lance's stand or mine; one of us would get the shot.

I secretly hoped it would be Lance so I wouldn't get the chance of screwing up, but it sounded like he was coming my way. There might be two bulls; maybe one has a cow with him because he is grunting almost continuously. One seemed closer than the other; I heard him crashing through the trees on the other side of the lake. Lance called again because it seemed the bull had turned away. He seemed to have crossed over the point of land on the other side, and I thought I could hear him in the water. I thought that the bull would swim across the narrows, make a shore right under Lance's stand and Lance will shoot him.

It didn't work out that way. When I saw him, he was on the far shore going in the opposite direction. Who knows what happened. Whatever the reason, he left the area, grunting all the way. While definitely a rutting bull, this one had not thrown all caution to the wind.

Ninety minutes later, Lance came over to my tree stand. I got down so we could talk because we don't speak above a whisper outside the cabin. It seemed likely that the bull—possibly more than one—had a cow with him, although Lance didn't see the cow. While the bull stood on the point, however, Lance noted that another animal had continued along the west side of the lake while making lots of noise but no grunts. Lance, thinking the bull was walking away, called again which brought the bull off the point, out of the woods and along the west shore where he kept following the other animal. It makes sense now. Lance's calling was good enough to bring the bull out; however, it's not surprising that the bull would not cross the lake to cavort with an unknown siren and let a cow he knew was about ready for breeding get away. He may be back!

It was time for us to move. Lance took his portable tree stand (I'd left mine at the lower end of Lake Francois) to Lake Claire, marking a trail with surveyor's tape so he wouldn't get lost coming back. I dropped him off at the southwest end of the table where the portage begins and paddled the canoe back to the narrows.

We had set up a water filter before I took Lance to the portage. When I returned, the glass was nearly full. I drank the water and set the glass under the dripping filter again so Lance could have a glass of cold water when he returned tonight. (We avoid drinking untreated lake water because of the possibility of contracting Giardia.)

The sun came out briefly at noon while I ate part of my lunch in the tree stand. There were no answers to the calls. Apparently, there are no bulls in this valley that surrounds Lake Francois.

Getting antsy, I got out of my stand about 3 p.m. and cleared some bushes so I would have a clear 30-yard shot to an old moose trail—apparently now abandoned. There was a scrape and an old pile of dung from a previous summer, but otherwise no signs of recent use. After another hour or so in the stand, I got down again and began making a trail to the lower end of the lake. This stopped when I cut a hole in my hip boot with the saw. Disgusted, I returned to the stand determined to sit it out. I fashioned a patch for the hole with Steri-Strips—the only thing I had in my day pack.

Moose hunting is much like army life: days and days of infinite boredom interrupted by moments of sheer horror (this is someone else's quote but the comparison is mine).

Two hours crept by, and then three. I did some practice calling, mostly to hear how I sounded. I now was anticipating picking up Lance and sharing an evening meal, even though I wasn't hungry because I had continued to nibble on my lunch. A hot meal and a warm sleeping bag

seemed to grow more desirable as the hours passed slowly. It was cloudy now and the wind stirred only briefly out of the southwest.

It may have been 6:30 p.m. or so when I heard the first, faint cow call out of the northwest, perhaps as far as the beaver meadow near camp. Until I heard the bull grunt, though, I thought other hunters had usurped our territory. Yes, it was a bull; the grunt is unmistakable, sounding like it's coming from the bottom of a 55-gallon drum. It sounded like he was with the cow, but these sounds are very deceptive. He could be responding to the cow's call or my call; I really don't know.

When I heard the bull, I either forgot about the cow or she stopped calling. The bull definitely was coming closer. He crashed through the trees. The path he followed was similar to that of the bull that had walked away this morning. Was the cow with him? Would this be a repeat performance? Was it the same bull? Would Lance get to the end of the portage and hear what was happening? Would darkness interfere? All these questions ran through my mind as I alternated listening and calling whenever he stopped for what seemed to be too long a time.

He seemed to be on the point but well back in the trees. I tried a little "oink" call that Father Deschenes had demonstrated many years ago. He was grunting and crashing again, grunting almost continuously with every other step he took. When he stopped, I "oinked" again. Once, he seemed to turn and move away. I decided to gamble by using the commercial call once again. Although experts will tell you never to change calls during a calling sequence, it worked. He seemed to be turning back toward me. The next time he stopped, I "oinked" with the birch bark horn, facing away from him. That brought him closer to the edge of the lake; once more did it!

He appeared out of the trees just north of the point and headed straight across the narrows toward me. I said a silent prayer that my arrow would fly true and find its mark. As he approached the shore, he turned toward the south. I brought the bow around to the other side of the tree. It would be neither a close nor an easy shot. The adrenaline-instilled shakes, which had continued all through this half-hour episode, suddenly ceased. I was

cool and steady as I drew back the bowstring, setting the
20-yard pin behind his shoulder and tracking him as he
moved from broadside to slightly quartering away.

Just as he was about to go behind some spruce trees
and out of sight, I released. I saw the arrow bury itself in
the right spot.

My prayer was answered because the shot was a good
one. The arrow did not penetrate fully, however, but I
hoped it had penetrated both lungs. I was using a
Thunderhead 100 broadhead for the first time this year on
an XX75-2319 arrow and a 73-pound Golden Eagle bow.
This was the acid test!

He ran straight toward Lance's stand site and stood in
the water out of sight. I cow-called to him to keep him
from walking or swimming away. It worked. He stood
there for a minute and then I heard him flounder. I was

sure it was over. But he fought to stand and then lunged into the water, swimming out into the lake. He had not gone far before the water was still.

I yelled to Lance, but there was no response. I grabbed a piece of stout rope and hurried out in the canoe. A small frisbee-sized piece of hair remained on the surface—it was his rump. Probing with the paddle, I located his antlers. Reaching into the water past my elbow, I fastened the rope to them. I tied a paddle to the other end of the rope and hurried to pick up Lance. It was almost dark and Lance wasn't at the landing. Had he shot a moose, too? We're only allowed one moose between us. It would be very embarrassing if we had two.

I found Lance standing in the trail, listening and watching. No, he hadn't shot a moose. I told Lance that we're going to have a real problem getting my moose out of the lake so we can butcher him.

His rump was still floating when we reached him. I tied the rope lashed to his head to the back of the canoe, and we towed him. The only problem was hauling him across the narrows because his legs dragged on the bottom.

We couldn't get the moose all the way to shore because the water was too shallow. We left it with its head on a rock and went back to camp in the dark to pick up tools and rope, and have some supper.

After eating, we hiked back to the bay, and found a spot where we could haul him out of the water. As he came out of the water, the size of his rack became apparent. He was a big one! I couldn't get my hand completely around his antler at its base. The paddles were high and at least 4 feet wide. It was truly an impressive sight.

It was 1 a.m. before we had him gutted and opened up for cooling. We found that the arrow had pierced one lung and the heart, stopping against the brisket. We finally made it to bed at 2:30 a.m.

Five hours later I was awake and writing in my journal, listening to the rain. If it doesn't quit, it will certainly complicate the butchering job.

After a huge breakfast, we were off to work. The rain stopped long enough for us to get the moose winched out of the bushes along the lakeshore, into the trees, and to get a tarp up over it. Rain fell intermittently the rest of the

day. A big tarp—this one is 15 x 30 feet and could be wider—is a basic necessity on a moose hunt; it seems to rain a lot during hunting season.

It took the rest of the day to quarter and transport all the meat about a mile back to camp. When we finished, we were too tired to eat supper so we went right to bed.

Friday morning, we cleaned up the site and hauled all the stuff to the landing. We transported four loads by canoe across the flooded beaver meadow, dropping the heavy loads near the beaver dam. Later we carried everything up the trail to our camp. We were done! It was just past noon.

I cut a pound or so of nice meat from inside the ribs, up under the hump—much like the tenderloins but farther forward. Smothered in onions and simmered in its own juices, served with string beans as a side dish, the meat provided a feast fit for nobility. We gorged ourselves, feeling good because we had accomplished so much. It was our reward for a job well done.

Later, Dave Chanda, N.J. Fish and Wildlife, scored the rack unofficially at 153 and 3/8. The minimum score for the Pope and Young record book is 135 points so this rack had no trouble qualifying.

I never thought I'd be a trophy hunter. The importance of the listing is secondary, however, to the real trophy—the memory of the hunt which returns whenever I see the rack on the wall.

Small Game Recipes

Smothered Rabbit

Serves: 2-3
Prep Time: 1 hour

1 medium to large rabbit
   seasoned flour
3 T. butter
3 onions, sliced
1 cup sour cream

Cut up rabbit into medium-sized pieces and dredge in seasoned flour. Saute rabbit in melted butter until browned. Cover thickly with sliced onions. Pour sour cream over rabbit. Cover and simmer for 1 hour or bake at 300 degrees for 1 hour.

Richard Anderson
Tunkhannock, Pennsylvania

Rabbit Stew

Serves: 4-5
Prep Time: 3 hours

1   rabbit, skinned and cut into small pieces
2   cups water
2   bay leaves
5   whole peppercorns
1   lb. carrots, sliced
1   bunch celery, diced
2   cups chicken broth
1¹/₂   lbs. potatoes, sliced
       salt and pepper to taste
¹/₃-¹/₂ cup flour

In large pot, combine all ingredients except flour. Cover and simmer for 2¹/₂-3 hours or until rabbit and potatoes are tender. Thicken sauce with flour.

Dan Murrell
Indianola, Missouri

Fried Rabbit

Serves: 2-3
Prep Time: 1 hour

 1   rabbit, cut into small pieces
 1   cup flour
 1   tsp. salt
 1   tsp. paprika
 1/8 tsp. pepper
     cooking oil
 1   can cream of mushroom soup
 1 1/2 cups milk

Mix flour, salt, paprika and pepper in paper bag. Shake rabbit pieces in bag. In large skillet, brown rabbit pieces in oil. Remove rabbit; drain fat. Add soup and milk to skillet. Heat on low setting for 45 minutes. Serve with noodles.

Gerard Daudier
Biddeford, Maine

Hunter's Ethics ...

Pass along to younger hunters the attitudes and skills essential to a true outdoorsman. Be cooperative and patient when hunting with youngsters.

Rabbit Cacciatore

Serves: 4
Prep Time: 1 hour

1	3-lb. rabbit, cut into serving-sized pieces
1/4	cup olive oil
1/2	cup flour
2	cups onions, chopped
1/2	cup mushrooms, sliced
1/2	cup green peppers, sliced
3	garlic cloves, crushed
1	16-oz. can tomatoes, drained
1	8-oz. can tomato sauce
1/4	cup white wine
1	bay leaf
1/2	tsp. oregano
1/4	tsp. basil

Rinse rabbit in cold water and dry. Add oil to skillet. Dredge rabbit meat in flour. Cook rabbit for 15 minutes; remove and set aside. Remove all remaining oil except 3 T. Add onions, mushrooms, green peppers and garlic. Cook over medium heat until tender. Add tomatoes, tomato sauce, wine, bay leaf, oregano and basil. Add rabbit and cook until tender, about 30-40 minutes. Serve with pasta or rice.

Stan Roesch
Harrisburg, Pennsylvania

Hunter's Safety ...

You should treat every firearm as if it were loaded, even when you think it is not.

Old-Fashioned Rabbit Stew

Serves: 4
Prep Time: 2 hours, 30 minutes

1-2	lbs. rabbit meat
1/4	cup all-purpose flour
1¹/4	tsp. salt
1/3	tsp. black pepper
1/4	tsp. dry mustard
1	T. vegetable oil
2¹/2	cups water
1	T. Worcestershire sauce
2	cups potatoes, sliced
1	cup onion, sliced
1	cup carrots, sliced
1/2	tsp. dill weed

Combine flour, salt, pepper and dry mustard in paper bag.
Slice meat in cubes and shake in bag to coat. Heat oil in
large skillet. Brown meat over medium heat, turning frequently. Remove meat and place in 2¹/2-qt. casserole; set
aside. Sprinkle flour mixture from bag into frying pan. Stir
vigorously until smooth. Add water slowly and stir. Add
Worcestershire sauce, cooking and stirring until smooth.
Pour mixture over rabbit. Cover and bake at 350 degrees for
1 hour, 30 minutes. Put vegetables into casserole and sprinkle dill weed over top. Cover and bake for 1 more hour or
until rabbit and vegetables are tender.

John Judd
Mason, Michigan

Rabbit Caruso And Rice

Serves: 3-4
Prep Time: 1 hour

2	rabbits, boned and cut into 2-inch pieces
	garlic salt and pepper to taste
3	T. butter or margarine
1	26-oz. jar spaghetti sauce
1/4	tsp. oregano
1/4	tsp. dried parsley flakes
1	T. instant minced onion
1	T. Worcestershire sauce
2	cups celery, sliced

Season rabbit with garlic salt and pepper. Saute rabbit in butter for 3-5 minutes. Stir in spaghetti sauce, oregano, parsley flakes, minced onion, Worcestershire sauce and celery. Cover and simmer for 10 minutes until celery is tender. Serve over rice with Parmesan cheese.

Gregory Morock
Corning, New York

Hunting Tip ...

Because white-tailed deer are more active at dawn or dusk, successful hunters need to be in position early enough and late enough in order to take advantage of this trait.

Delicious Rabbit

Serves: 3-4
Prep Time: 10 hours

1	rabbit, cut into serving-sized pieces
1/2	cup flour
	cooking oil
1 1/2	tsp. salt
1/8	tsp. pepper
1	bottle barbecue sauce
1	cup water

Soak rabbit in salted water for 6-8 hours; drain. Dredge rabbit pieces in flour. Fry in hot oil until golden brown. Add salt, pepper and barbecue sauce. Put in baking dish. Add 1 cup water and bake at 350 degrees for 2 hours until tender.

Willis Coblentz
Hartley, Delaware

Pita Rabbit

Serves: 4-6
Prep Time: 1-2 hours

1-2	rabbits
1	bottle barbecue sauce
	liquid smoke
	water
4-6	pita-bread pockets

Cook and bone rabbit. Put rabbit in Crockpot and cover with barbecue sauce, thinning with water if needed. Add liquid smoke as desired. Cook for 1-2 hours. Serve in pita-bread pockets.

John Richardson
Springfield, Illinois

Maple Rabbit Casserole

Serves: 4-5
Prep Time: 1 hour

1	rabbit, quartered
2	T. olive oil
1	cup onion, chopped
2	T. Worchestershire sauce
2	T. chili powder
1/4	cup apple cider vinegar
1 1/2-2	cups maple syrup
	your favorite hot sauce (optional)

In frying pan, brown rabbit in olive oil. Place rabbit in casserole and set aside. In saucepan, combine remaining ingredients and warm over low heat for 3 minutes. Pour mixture over rabitt and bake (covered) at 350 degrees for 45-60 minutes. Uncover and allow to brown for 5 minutes before serving. Serve over rice or noodles.

Dianne Rowland
Glennie, Michigan

Hunting Tip ...

If you're hunting from a tree stand in camo gear, make sure anything that is bright (like socks) or reflective (like rings or glasses) is adequately covered.

Hasenpfeffer

Serves: 6
Prep Time: 1 hour

1	3-lb. rabbit	1/4	tsp. pepper
2	T. butter	1	T. mustard seed
2	T. bacon, chopped	1	onion, chopped
2	carrots, chopped	1/4	cup canned
1	bay leaf		mushrooms
8	cloves	1	cup water
1	garlic clove	1	cup cream
1	tsp. salt		

Clean rabbit, cutting meat from bones. In saucepan, melt butter and add all ingredients, except cream. Cover and simmer for about 1 hour until meat is tender. Mix in cream and serve.

Donald Bollinger
South Bend, Indiana

Virginia Fried Breakfast

Serves: 1
Prep Time: 20-30 minutes

2	serving-sized pieces small-game meat
2	eggs
	salt and pepper to taste
2-3	cups flour
	cooking oil

Beat eggs in large bowl. Season meat with salt and pepper and add to egg mixture. Stir until eggs fully cover meat. Dredge meat in flour, coating thoroughly. Heat oil in fying pan until hot. Fry meat over medium heat until golden brown. Carefully pour in enough water to cover meat; cover and cook until liquid makes gravy covering half of meat. Serve meat with gravy and biscuits.

Bill Hardee
Norfolk, Virginia

Sunny Lake Rabbit

Serves: 4
Prep Time: 1 hour, 40 minutes

  1   rabbit, quartered
      meat tenderizer
      garlic salt to taste
      salt and pepper to taste
      cooked rice
  2   cans cream of mushroom soup
  1   large bag of frozen vegetables
  1   can water chestnuts
      soy sauce

Season rabbit parts and set aside for 20-30 minutes. Cook rice and set aside. Brown meat in frying pan for 3-4 minutes. Layer rice, 1 can mushroom soup and rabbit in casserole. Add vegetables, water chestnuts and mushrooms. Spread last can of mushroom soup evenly over top. Cover casserole with aluminum foil and bake at 350 degrees for 45-60 minutes. Serve with soy sauce.

Dianne Rowland
Glennie, Michigan

Hunting Tip ...

When choosing camo patterns, try to match the pattern to the background. Also, try wearing pants in one pattern and a shirt or jacket in another pattern.

Squirrel Pie

Serves: 5
Prep Time: 3 hours

2	squirrels, skinned
1	cup carrots, sliced
1	cup celery, diced
1	cup mushrooms, sliced
1	cup potatoes, peeled and cubed
1¹/2	cups water
	cornstarch
1	pie shell (2 crusts)

Boil squirrels in salted water until done. Remove from heat and cool. Pick meat from bones. Add squirrel meat and vegetables to 1¹/2 cups boiling water; simmer until vegetables are tender. Slowly add cornstarch to thicken and simmer. Pour cooled vegetable mixture and squirrel meat into pie shell. Cover with additional crust and slit vents with knife. Bake at 360 degrees for 50-60 minutes. Cover edges with aluminum foil to prevent burning.

Paul Skolaski
De Forest, Wisconsin

Hunting Tip ...

Mature bucks prefer to sit tight or sneak away, rather than run. Stop often and look all around you. If you don't, you could walk right past one.

Jeff's Squirrel Stew

Serves: 6
Prep Time: 3 hours, 10 minutes

2	squirrels, cut into stew meat
1/2	lb. salt pork
1	onion, minced
2¹/2	cups lima beans
5	corn ears, shaved
5	potatoes (whole)
1/2	tsp. pepper
2	tsp. sugar
4	cups sliced tomatoes or 2 cups picante sauce
1/2	lb. butter
	flour

Bring 4 qts. salted water to a boil. Add pork, onion, lima beans, corn, potatoes, pepper and squirrels. Cover and simmer for 2 hours. Add sugar and tomatoes. Cover and simmer for 1 more hour. Cut butter into almond-sized balls and roll in flour. Place balls in stew and cover. Bring stew to a boil and cook for 7-10 minutes, stirring twice. Serve.

Jeff Dolick
San Antonio, Texas

Hunter's Safety ...

When you have finished hunting, unload your gun before returning to your vehicle or camp. Double-check the gun before storing it at home.

Stuffed Squirrel

Serves: 2
Prep Time: 1 hour, 15 minutes

1	large gray squirrel, skinned and cleaned
1¹/2	cups stuffing mix
1	garlic clove, minced
1	medium onion, chopped
2	T. spicy brown mustard
2	T. Tabasco sauce
¹/2	cup flour
1	lb. fresh mushrooms, sliced
2	cups chicken broth

Parboil squirrel for 10 minutes. Combine dry stuffing mix, garlic, onion, mustard, Tabasco sauce and flour to form stuffing. Put stuffing in cavity of squirrel and place in roasting pan. Add sliced mushrooms to chicken broth and pour broth over squirrel, thoroughly saturating stuffing. Cover pan tightly with aluminum foil and bake at 350 degrees for approximately 1 hour or until tender.

Greg Zimmerlee
Leitchfield, Kentucky

Hunter's Safety ...

Never attempt to use a permanent stand that you do not thoroughly trust; it may be rickety or contain rotten wood that could collapse from your weight.

Raccoon Stew

Serves: varies
Prep Time: 2-4 hours

>   raccoon meat
>   water
>   potatoes, chopped
>   carrots, chopped
> 1   pkg. stew seasoning
>   salt and pepper to taste
>   celery, chopped

Cut meat into chunks and brown in skillet. Then combine
remaining ingredients in large stew pot; add meat. Cover
and cook for 2-4 hours on low heat.

Kerry Schoenborn
Molalla, Oregon

Armadillo Sausage

Serves: varies
Prep Time: 2 hours

3-4	lbs. armadillo with 7 kernels (glands) removed from forelegs and hindlegs	5	large garlic cloves
		1	medium onion
		4	bay leaves, crushed
1/2	lb. fresh pork fat	1	tsp. thyme
1	tsp. ground coriander	2	tsp. red pepper, crushed
1	tsp. salt	1	tsp. black pepper

Mix all ingredients and pass through coarse cutter (grinder)
once, distributing seasonings evenly. Pass through grinder
again. Stuff into casings and cool-smoke for 2 hours at 60-
85 degrees.

S. J. Bellofatto
Columbus, Georgia

Oven-Roasted Groundhog

Serves: 4-6
Prep Time: 8 hours

2　groundhogs (whole)
　　Morton Tender Quick
$3/4$　cup vinegar
$1/4$　cup soy sauce
1　cup water
2　large onions, chopped
2　garlic cloves, minced
　　your favorite seasonings
1　lb. fresh mushrooms, sliced

Combine Morton Tender Quick, vinegar, soy sauce, water, onions and garlic cloves to form marinade. Marinate groundhogs for 4 hours in refrigerator, turning after 2 hours. Place meat and marinade mixture in cast-iron skillet or Dutch oven. Generously sprinkle your favorite seasonings over meat and cover tightly. Bake for 2-4 hours at 300 degrees until meat separates easily with fork. Add mushrooms 30 minutes before removing from oven. Serve with potatoes.

Todd Eckles
Hopedale, Ohio

Hunter's Safety ...

Never sit or stand in a tree stand without some kind of safety belt attached to the tree. If you slip, the strap may prevent some broken bones.

Turtle Bake

Serves: 3-4
Prep Time: 2 hours

2	cups turtle meat	$1^3/4$	cups water
3-4	tsp. butter	1	pkg. frozen mixed
1	onion, diced		vegetables
	salt and pepper to taste		

Brown meat in butter. Add onion, salt, pepper and water.
Simmer for 1 hour; drain water. Put in greased casserole
adding vegetables. Bake at 350 degrees for 30 minutes until
brown. Serve with biscuits, fried onion rings or tater tots.

Robert J. Carl
Blue Earth, Minnesota

Turtle Soup

Serves: several
Prep Time: 6 hours

2	lbs. ground turtle meat		carrots
1	chicken	6	hardboiled eggs
2	lbs. ground beef	4	T. lemon juice
1	pt. peas	$1/4$	lb. butter
1	pt. corn	3	T. Tabasco sauce
$3^1/2$	pts. catsup	1	T. pepper
$3^1/2$	large onions	8	T. salt
7	celery stalks	$1^1/2$	oz. pickle spice
$1/2$	cabbage head	8	oz. noodles
	potatoes	5	gals. water
	green beans		

Cook turtle, chicken and beef then put meat through
grinder. Chop vegetables and eggs. Combine all ingredients
in large stew pot. Cook for 4-5 hours until meat and vegetables are tender. Serve.

Don Bollinger
South Bend, Indiana

Puerco-Espin (Porcupine)

Serves: varies
Prep Time: 1 hour, 15 minutes

1 porcupine, cleaned and quartered
1 large onion, sliced
1 garlic clove, minced
1 bay leaf
1 cup parsley or cilantro, chopped
3 T. shortening
1 cup potatoes, julienned
1 cup carrots, sliced
1 cup celery, chopped
2 cups porcupine broth
1 cup tomato sauce
4 T. flour
4 T. water
2 tsp. salt
1 thyme sprig
1 basil sprig

Cover meat with water. Add salt, half of onion, garlic, bay leaf and parsley. Cook until tender; drain, saving broth and vegetables. Discard bay leaf. Bone and dice meat when cool. Melt shortening in skillet. Add potatoes, carrots, celery and remaining onion. Cover and cook on low heat for 15 minutes. Add broth and tomato sauce, bringing to a boil. Blend flour, water and salt until smooth. Add flour mixture to skillet to thicken. Then add all ingredients to skillet. Reduce heat and simmer until vegetables are tender.

S. J. Bellofatto
Columbus, Georgia

Muskrat Chili

Serves: 4-6
Prep Time: 2-3 hours

3   muskrats, ground or cut into chunks
3   large onions, grated
3   garlic cloves, grated
1   qt. whole tomatoes (with water)
2-3 cans kidney beans (with liquid)
     chili powder to taste

Skin muskrats and remove all glands and fat. Parboil muskrats and 1 onion for 45 minutes. Remove meat from bones and grind or cut into small chunks. In skillet, brown meat, adding onions and garlic. Then add remaining ingredients and simmer at medium heat for 1 hour.

Bill Bauman
McKeesport, Pennsylvania

Possum Stew

Serves: 3-6
Prep Time: 6-9 hours

2   opossums
1   large onion, diced
3   potatoes, chopped
4   carrots, chopped
3   celery stalks (including tops), chopped

2   garlic cloves, diced
1/4 tsp. oregano
1   tsp. parsley
    water

Skin and quarter opossum, removing all glands and fat. Parboil meat and onion for 45 minutes. Remove meat from bones and place in Crockpot. Add remaining ingredients and enough water to fill Crockpot. Cook on low setting for 8-10 hours or on high setting for 4-6 hours.

Bill Bauman
McKeesport, Pennsylvania

My Favorite Small Game Recipe

Recipe Name   ————————————————
Serves   ————————————————
Prep Time   ————————————————

Ingredients

———————————   ———————————
———————————   ———————————
———————————   ———————————
———————————   ———————————
———————————   ———————————
———————————   ———————————
———————————   ———————————
———————————   ———————————

Directions

————————————————————————
————————————————————————
————————————————————————
————————————————————————
————————————————————————
————————————————————————
————————————————————————
————————————————————————
————————————————————————
————————————————————————
————————————————————————

Grandpa And Billy— Hunting Partners!

By Jim Shockey

I f Grandpa were here now, he'd hear Billy's name and you wouldn't be able to stop him—he'd be off on some story. I can here him now. "What's that you say about my buddy, Billy, and me?"

He'd cock his head to the side and start in—even if you didn't want him to.

"Well, we been huntin' partners for as long as I can remember. Them guys who grow apart over the years? Billy and I, we never could figure it. Hell, we ain't even hardly been apart a day, not even once, for the last 20 years or so. Just like an old shoe that Billy.

Look at him snoring up a storm in the corner, sitting there in that creaky old rocking chair. Funny how time plays tricks on a guy, I always remember that chair being in the other corner, under the moose head. Fact is, things have changed a bit. Just have to lean back and look up to see that. Time was when those heavy rafters could have held 20 feet of snow. Don't think they could hardly hold up another spider web now.

But here, let me tell you a story. It was just last week. Billy was sleeping right there in that old chair and I got this urge to do a little work on the lodge.

"Hey, Billy!" I said, getting up and shuffling over to give Billy a jab in the ribs. "Wake up!"

"Huh?" He was pretty groggy. "Who's there?"

"Wake up, old hunting buddy. I think it's time we changed those rafters. What's it been? Fifty years?"

Billy can't see too good any more. Until he puts on his glasses, he kinda squints-like.

"Rafters?" he said, rubbing his eyes. "Fifty years? Or was it yesterday?"

I knew what he meant. It did seem only yesterday Billy and I strained and grunted for a whole summer. Figure it was lucky both of us didn't lose our wives that year.

"Sundown comes this evening sometime. Sure would be nice to get it part way done," I said.

Billy worked his glasses on. "Yeah," he agreed. "Expect you're right. We best be gettin' to it."

"I'll go get the hammer and nails," I offered as I sat myself down on our tattery overstuffed couch.

"You do that," Billy agreed. "And I'll go start peelin' us some logs."

With that settled, both of us leaned back, Billy into the rocker and me into the couch—to conserve energy for the task at hand.

Conserving energy. Me and Billy do a lot of that these days. I don't suppose we have been on a trail for quite a few long years now. No. We just like to putter around the lodge, do what we can: a little cooking; fix a bit.

"When was the last time we hunted, Billy? Sixty-four?"

Billy squinted at me through his glasses.

"No. No, I think it was '66."

"Yeah, maybe you're right," I said. "That was the year we decided alcohol and hunting didn't mix."

"Yep," Billy agreed. "Left our guns at home."

We didn't drink much really. Not so you'd notice. In fact, the only thing we did drink was hot apple juice and rum with a stick of cinnamon. Naw. That wasn't the real reason we quit hunting. It was more like, the purpose of hunting is to make memories. So when a guy's mind gets filled up, there just doesn't seem to be much use in hunting anymore, not as far as we're concerned anyway.

"Hey, I have an idea, Billy. Maybe before we get to work we should have a glass of that hot apple juice and rum. Just like we used to."

"Yeah," he nodded his head. "With a stick of cinnamon, too."

"That's the one. I'll make it," I said as I pulled myself off the couch and hobbled over to the wood stove.

"While you're doing that, I'll clean up some of these hunting magazines. Been laying around for years," Billy said as he reached over to the end table beside him.

I knew Billy wouldn't be doing much cleaning. He never moved from that rocking chair, lest it was absolutely necessary. I almost dropped the apple juice when Billy let out a holler behind me.

"Whoo-wee! Come and take a look at this."

I knew it had to be important for Billy to whoop it up like that. Over the last bunch of years Billy hadn't done much whoopin', or uppin' for that matter.

"Lookit this! Remember!" Billy was excited.

"You be careful not to get too hepped up, Billy," I warned. "Now what's all this about?"

It was an old magazine, from 1948. Most of the pictures were drawings. The front cover showed a man with a shotgun, hiding inside a huge hollow goose.

"Remember? That was the year they came out with those giant decoys you could hide inside," Billy said. "That was our idea. We thought of it a year earlier, remember?"

I had to admit I remembered all right. Billy and I always figured we lost a million dollars because we didn't capitalize on our idea; 'course, our idea wasn't exactly the same.

"Touch wood we never blow another opportunity like that again," Billy said as he rapped his knuckles against the table beside him.

Before I could agree, Billy looked up like he heard something.

"Who's there?" he said. We both listened but nobody answered.

"Must have been squirrels," I said.

"Yeah," Billy agreed. "Squirrels."

"Where's that old photo album of ours, Billy?" I asked,

sifting through the magazines, now ragged and yellowed.

"Got it right here," he said, opening it carefully so as not to spill the rum and apple juice I had set beside him. Billy flipped through the ragged and curled-up pages until he came to the picture we both knew was there.

"That's it!" I said, pointing. It was black-and-white documented proof of our idea. The date in the corner read October 1947.

"Was that 40 years ago? Or was it yesterday?" Billy asked as he looked over at me.

I knew what he meant. Seemed only yesterday Billy called me up on the oak phone that used to hang on the wall in the kitchen.

"Huntin' buddy!" he had yelled into the phone. "Don't move an inch. I got us an idea!"

Now we had already hunted together for a handful of years by then and I knew one of Billy's ideas this close to hunting season could only mean trouble. I didn't have long to wait to find out though because it wasn't 20 minutes later that Billy pulled up in his Model T. I suppose if I had started running the instant Billy hung up, I might have got away but he woulda found me.

"Well? What's this big idea?" I rolled my eyes upward.

"Hang on, my friend, all in good time." Billy was enjoying the moment. "Remember back in the war?"

"I try not to," I answered.

"Remember how we used to have those fancy camouflage duds? Could barely see each other when we used to sneak around in the woods."

"Yeah, so?" I rolled my eyes again.

"Remember how we always figured those duds would be the cat's meow during deer season back home?" Billy leaned an elbow back on the hood of his car and tipped his hat so he was looking at me down his nose.

"Yeah," I said.

"Well, you'll never guess what I just bought down at ole Doc Williams' estate sale."

"You got us a couple pairs of that camouflage stuff?" I guessed.

"Nope," Billy smiled. "I was sittin' there knowing I wouldn't be able to afford anything anyway when these came up." He twisted around and pulled two bulging bags

looking like somebody's dirty laundry from off the seat.

"Wonderful," I said. "What are they?"

"All in good time, my impatient friend, all in good time." He looked down his nose at me again. "Those army duds are good but I figured we would still look unnatural. The trick is to look like something the deer might see every day back in the bush."

"I agree, so what?"

"Well, back in the old country, the Doc must have attended a few masquerade balls."

I was getting awfully worried about Billy's idea.

"I got a pile of chores to do," I said, trying to get away.

"Oh, no you don't. Here try this on." Billy shoved a bag in my hand.

Five minutes later I stepped out from behind the out-house.

"There!" Billy said as he held his hands out to me. "How do you feel?"

"Like a dope," I said.

"Don't you feel any different at all?" he asked.

"Funny," I answered. "Very funny."

"There, there," he said. "When have you ever seen a big buck run away from a duck?"

"A duck?" I said.

"Ya, you know, a duck. Quack, quack." Billy put a friendly arm around my shoulders. "The kind you see sittin' on the river right where that big buck comes down to drink every day.

"Never mind," Billy said. "Here, I'll put mine on."

Five minutes later he reappeared. "Guess what I am."

"A buzzard?" I said through the large duck bill tied to my face.

"Droll," he said. "Very droll, but you're wrong. I am a wise, old owl."

"You get to be a wise, old owl and I get to be a duck?"

"Seems only fair," he said. "Hoo-hoo."

"Quack, quack," I replied.

Billy jabbed me in the ribs with his bony finger. I looked up from the pages of the photo album to see Billy tuck both hands into his arm pits while he flapped his elbows up and down.

"Hoo-hoo!" he hooted. "Hoo-hoo!"

Actually, the sound coming from Billy's lips was more like "Ooo-ooo." He refused to wear his teeth while he was in the lodge.

"Quack, quack!" I joined in and flapped my arms up and down. I quacked and flapped around the room, from log wall to log wall. In my younger years it might have been an effort to waddle but now it was easy.

Billy ooo'ed and I quacked until we had tears in our eyes. Exhausted, I flopped back on the couch.

"Touch wood we never act as dumb as we did back then." Billy rapped his knuckles on the table.

I was about to agree when Billy wrinkled up his forehead and looked toward the door. "Who's there?"

No one answered.

"Must have been the shutters in the wind," I said.

"Yeah, shutters." Billy wiped the corner of his eye.

We both looked down at the photo album.

"Never did get our deer that year," I said.

"Yeah," Billy said. "Remember?"

Billy drove into my yard two hours before daybreak on opening day. I did not bother turning the porch light on, him being an owl and all. He really did look more like a buzzard than an owl, though, especially when he appeared in the doorway without his feathered owl mask on. I could see he was excited.

"You've got that look in your eye again." I started to pull away.

"Well, old hunting buddy," Billy exclaimed as he put his friendly wing around me like a hook, "I've been working all week on a project that will make your hunt a snap."

I bent over to pull on my papier-mache' webbed feet. "I don't think I want to hear this," I said.

"Nonsense, my boy, wait till you see what I have in the car. Here, let me help you tie that to your face."

Owl feet are easier to walk in so Billy beat me to the car. He had a large object pulled off the roof by the time I got there. It looked like a bunch of branches but, on closer inspection, I saw it was a large rubber inner tube with willows tied to it. I gave Billy a puzzled look.

"That is your waterproof nest, my friend." Billy tucked his wing tips in his belt and rocked back on his heels.

"Nest?" I asked. "Waterproof?"

"Yep. Got it figured this way." He reached into the car and pulled out a brick which had a rope wrapped around it. "You get in your nest and I put you out in the water. You anchor yourself and when that big buck comes down, you shoot him."

"Where's your nest?" I asked.

"Don't need one. I'll sneak downstream 'bout a mile or so and climb a tree," he said.

First light found us at the water's edge. Billy was standing and I was sitting in the nest with my papier-mache' feet sticking over the side. "Here's your anchor. Just don't miss."

"Cast off!" I said as Billy gave me a good shove.

"Hoo-hoo!" Billy said as he disappeared into the forest.

"Quack! Quack!" I replied.

I listened to Billy hooting all the way downstream as I

slowly drifted well away from shore. When I decided I was far enough out, I tied the end of the anchor rope to the inner tube and heaved the brick as far as I could out into the water, intending to let the brick's momentum unravel the rope. It did so nicely and the brick still had enough momentum to carry another 20 feet past where the end of the rope hit the water. My good buddy Billy had forgotten to tie the rope to the brick. I was about to curse him when I noticed three things. The first was the glint of the rising sun off the barrel of my gun which I had left on shore. The second was the noticeable increase in speed as I drifted into midstream. The third had to do with Billy's water-proofing. It felt like somebody with icy fingers was reaching down the back of my underwear.

I suppose it took about two hours to float downstream to a point where I thought I might find Billy. I would have called to him but I knew my voice would be drowned out by the crows, cawing as they circled around an oak tree by the water's edge. As I drew near, I realized why they were so upset. There, sitting in the tree, was the biggest, ugliest buzzard I had ever seen in my life. The buzzard looked over in my direction, and I quickly realized it must be Billy—even though I did not remember his costume hav-ing white blotches and streaks all over it.

"Hoo-hoo," he said rather sadly.

"You look pooped!" I smiled at him as I floated by. "Yessiree, Billy! One heck of an idea."

As I was about to pass out of earshot, I yelled at Billy to get the car and catch me at the bridge further downstream. By then, my rear end was submerged in 6 inches of water. I was so miserable I didn't even notice the duck hunters sit-ting in a blind at the edge of the river until I was almost across from them.

"Wow! Will you look at the size of that one!" I heard one of them say."What in the hell is it?"

"Too ugly to be a swan," I heard a second voice say.

"Must be a honker! A Canada goose! Never seen one up close before," the first hunter said. "Let's blast it!"

Realizing the mortal danger I was in, I tried frantically to undo the knot holding the duck bill to my face.

"We can't just shoot him while he's sitting on his nest.

It wouldn't be sporting," one of the hunters said. "He has to fly."

Thank God the hunters in those days had ethics. I gave up trying to untie my duck bill and grabbed it by the top and bottom lips. Pulling it open, I yelled to the hunters, "I'm not a goose, you morons. I'm a duck—and, besides, I can't fly."

This confused the hunters for a moment. They looked at each other and then back at me. "Can you run?" one of them called out as if I had anywhere to run anyways.

By then I was out of shotgun range and I was happy when I spotted that 200-pound buzzard hanging from the bridge. Boy, that was funny, both of us hanging there. Billy laughed so hard he almost let go of my wing.

I looked over at Billy.

"Was it 40 years ago? Or was it yesterday?" Billy asked.

I knew what he meant. "I sure am glad we stopped that motorist and had him snap our picture, Billy. Means a lot, this old photo album."

We both sank back and looked around the room. Yes, it sure had changed. Seemed smaller now and I always remember there being a fireplace in the far corner. Billy noticed it, too, I am sure. His mouth was moving up and down but there weren't any sounds coming out. I knew what he was trying to say.

"Touch wood we still got each other, old hunting buddy." I rapped my knuckles against the table. Both of us looked toward the door.

"Mr. Shockey?"

I reached over and put a hand on my good friend Billy's shoulder. "I guess I got to be going now. Sure was nice to see you again, Billy. We'll have to fix those rafters tomorrow."

"Tomorrow," Billy agreed.

The door opened.

"Mr. Shockey? Bedtime now. I knocked a few times but I suppose you were talking to your friend Billy again and didn't hear me. Here, let me help you with that. Oh my, what a funny picture. That must be you there but who's that in the buzzard outfit? Oh, never mind. I'll wheel you to the bathroom now and help you put your pajamas on."

It's nice—the darkness, and the quiet. Used to be the

dark made me uneasy. It was alien. Now, somehow it seems inviting almost.

"Billy?" I whispered. "Billy? Are you there?"

"Ya, I'm here, " he said.

I knew he would be. I could hear that old rocking chair creaking under the moose head.

"Good night, Billy, " I whispered.

"Good night, old hunting buddy," he replied.

Good night, Grandpa.

Salads,
Appetizers &
Side Dishes

Coleslaw Supreme

Serves: 10-12
Prep Time: 15 minutes

$3/4$ cup mayonnaise
$33/4$ T. sugar
$21/4$ tsp. prepared mustard
2   tsp. onion, minced
$1/2$ tsp. salt
$1/3$ tsp. celery seed
1   lb. shredded cabbage
$1/2$ cup carrots, shredded

In bowl, blend mayonnaise, sugar and seasonings. Pour mixture over cabbage and carrots; mix thoroughly. Refrigerate for 1-2 hours before serving. (You can substitute 1-lb. pkg. pre-shredded coleslaw mix for cabbage and carrots.)

Avocado-Tomato Vinaigrette

Serves: several
Prep Time: 15-25 minutes

1-2   large tomatoes, sliced
1   ripe avocado, peeled and sliced
$1/2$ cup olive oil
1   T. lemon juice
1   T. wine vinegar
1   tsp. Grey Poupon mustard
$1/4$ tsp. ground black pepper
$1/4$ tsp. salt
$1/2$ tsp. garlic, minced

On large plate, arrange sliced tomato and avocado in layers. Whisk remaining ingredients in bowl and pour over tomato and avocado slices. Serve immediately.

Chinese Noodle Salad

Serves: several
Prep Time: 45 minutes

$1/4$	lb. butter
2	pkgs. dried noodles (Ramen)
$1/2$	cup sunflower seeds
$1/2$	cup almonds, slivered
1	head napa cabbage, cored and chopped into bite-sized pieces
5	green onions, sliced

Dressing:
1	cup salad oil
$3/4$	cup sugar
$1/2$	cup white vinegar
1	T. soy sauce
$1/2$	tsp. garlic salt

Over medium heat, melt butter in skillet. Break noodles into pieces and add to butter, stirring until browned. Add sunflower seeds and almonds. Saute for 4-6 minutes. Remove from heat. Combine dressing ingredients, mixing well. In large salad bowl, mix cabbage, onions, noodles and nuts. Pour dressing over salad and toss before serving.

Hunter's Safety ...

Always unload your gun before climbing a steep bank, traveling across slippery ground or crossing a stream or fence.

Hot Venison Strips

Serves: several
Prep Time: 40 minutes

     venison flank steak, sliced into thin strips
1   cup flour
     black pepper
2   eggs, beaten
1   cup bread crumbs
1   T. seasoned salt
1/2 tsp. celery seed
1   tsp. dry mustard powder
1/4 tsp. cayenne pepper
1/2 tsp. garlic powder
1/2 tsp. onion powder
     vegetable or olive oil

On plate, mix flour and black pepper. In bowl, beat eggs and set aside. On separate plate, mix bread crumbs with remaining seasonings. Rinse venison strips and dry well on paper towels. Roll each slice through flour until well-coated. Dip slices into egg mixture, drain and dredge in bread crumbs until completely covered. Place on paper towels and dry for 10-15 minutes.

In large frying pan, heat 1/4 inch oil until loose bread crumbs sizzle. Put breaded venison strips in oil and brown each side. Remove strips from oil and drain on paper towels. Serve hot. Dip strips in your favorite prepared sauce— sweet and sour, hot mustard or barbecue.

Mini Venison Pizzas

Serves: several
Prep Time: 20 minutes

	venison, ground
1-2	canned biscuits
	pizza sauce or tomato sauce
	mozzarella cheese, grated
1	green pepper, chopped
1	onion, chopped
	Parmesan cheese, grated
	olives (black and green), chopped

Brown venison in pan and set aside. Split open biscuits and separate dough. Roll each biscuit-dough serving by hand or with rolling pin until flat. Place flattened dough servings on cookie sheet and spread pizza sauce over each serving. Sprinkle venison over each serving and add other ingredients to taste. Bake at 350 degrees until cheese bubbles and browns slightly.

Wild Bird Dip

Serves: several
Prep. Time: 4-5 hours

3-4	gizzards (any game bird)	$1/4$	cup dry sherry
2-4	whole mushrooms		or red cooking wine
2	T. butter or margarine		salt and pepper
	celery salt	$1/2$	cup mayonnaise
	dried oregano		

Clean gizzards and boil in water until done (20-30 minutes, depending upon size); chop finely. Chop mushrooms and saute in butter with chopped giblets. Add celery salt and oregano to taste; stir well. Add sherry or wine, lower heat and simmer until wine is reduced almost completely. Add salt and pepper to taste. Put mayonnaise in bowl and add giblet mixture, mixing well. Refrigerate for 3-4 hours. Serve with chips or snack crackers.

Tracy's Secret Special Salsa

Serves: several
Prep Time: 30 minutes

1	16-oz. can tomato sauce
1	medium white onion, chopped
1	tsp. dried oregano
1	tsp. cumin
1	tsp. chopped garlic
1	tsp. onion powder
1	tsp. rosemary
1	tsp. thyme
1	T. fresh cilantro, chopped
2-6	jalapenos (store-bought jar)
1/3	cup juice from jar of jalapenos
1	32-oz. can stewed tomatoes

In food processor or blender, combine half of tomato
sauce, half of onion, half of spices, 2 jalapeno peppers and
half of jalapeno juice. Add half of stewed tomatoes. Blend
on low speed to avoid thin salsa. Pour salsa into mason
jars. Repeat procedure to make hot salsa, using 4 jalapenos
instead of 2. Keep salsa refrigerated. Pour salsa into dishes
and dip with tortilla chips.

Ultimate Nachos

Serves: several
Prep Time: 20 minutes

1	pkg. corn tortillas (5-6" in diameter)
1	cup cheddar or cojack cheese, chopped
1/2	cup black olives, chopped
1/4	cup jalapeno peppers, chopped
2	T. cilantro, chopped

Preheat oven to broil. Combine cheese, black olives,
jalapenos and cilantro. Mix until well-blended and finely
chopped. Place corn tortillas on baking sheet and coat
each with cheese mixture. Broil until cheese is bubbling.
Serve hot.

Crab Toast

Serves: several
Prep Time: 20 minutes

> 1 7-oz. pkg. frozen crab, shells removed
> 1/4 lb. margarine or butter
> 1 small jar old English cheese spread
> 1 1/2 tsp. mayonnaise
> 1/2 tsp. garlic salt
> 1/2 tsp. seasoned salt
> 1 pkg. English muffins or rye party loaf

Let margarine and cheese spread stand at room temperature until soft. Mix together. Combine cheese mixture with remaining ingredients and spread on English muffin halves or bread slices. Broil until cheese bubbles and turns slightly brown. Serve hot.

Glory-Ous Chip Dip

Serves: several
Prep Time: 15 minutes

> 1 8-oz. pkg. cream cheese
> 1/2 tsp. onion salt
> 1/2 tsp. garlic salt
> dash Worcestershire sauce
> 1 tsp. onion juice
> 1 tsp. garlic juice
> 1/4 cup catsup
> milk

Soften cream cheese and blend with remaining ingredients (except milk) in blender or with mixer. Add small amount of milk to make dip creamier. Taste and adjust ingredients as needed. Chill and serve with potato chips.

Shrimp/Crab Dip

Serves: several
Prep Time: 15 minutes

1	small can shrimp or crab meat, drained
1/2	8-oz. pkg. cream cheese
1/4	tsp. salt
1/2	tsp. ground black pepper
1	T. catsup
1	T. ground horseradish
	dash cayenne pepper

Soften cream cheese and blend with remaining ingredients. Serve with rye crackers, French bread slices or stone-ground saltines.

Mexican Bounty

Serves: several
Prep Time: 2-4 hours

1/2	8-oz. pkg. cream cheese
2-4	jalapeno peppers (seeds removed), chopped
1/4	cup black olives, chopped
1/4	cup green olives, chopped
2	T. salsa
1	tsp. cilantro, chopped (optional)
1/2	tsp. garlic, minced
1/4	tsp. cayenne pepper powder
1/4	tsp. cumin

Soften cream cheese and blend with remaining ingredients. Chill in refrigerator for 2-4 hours. Serve cold with tortilla chips.

Stuffed Artichokes

Serves: varies
Prep Time: 1 hour

1   large artichoke per person
    bread crumbs, seasoned to taste
    Parmesan cheese, grated
    butter
    garlic, minced

Pull off outer leaves of artichokes and slice off bases about
1/4 inch below stems. Put artichokes on sides and cut tops
off, leaving flat areas on top of artichokes. Clip off pointy
ends of each leaf. Combine bread crumbs and Parmesan
cheese (in equal proportions); set aside. Gently pull individual leaves out to make spaces between each layer and
sprinkle bread crumb mixture to fill spaces. Repeat for all
leaves. When finished, melt butter and drizzle over artichokes, soaking bread-crumb mixture between each layer
of leaves.

In saucepan, bring 1 inch of lightly salted water to a boil.
Place artichokes, stem-side down, in water and cover pan.
Boil for 30-40 minutes, checking frequently and adding
water to keep artichokes from burning. Remove to paper
towels to drain for a few minutes and serve in bowls or on
saucers.

To make dip, melt butter in small saucepan over medium
heat and add fresh minced garlic. Pull individual leaves
from artichokes and place root end in your mouth, holding outer edge. Pull out while gently biting leaf, pulling
bread crumb mixture as well as meat from leaf. Discard
remains of leaf. Dip in butter for added flavor. When all
except smallest leaves have been eaten, spoon out remaining leaves and fuzzy parts. The bases (artichoke hearts) can
be cut into quarters, dipped in butter and eaten.

Deep-Fried Wontons

Serves: several
Prep Time: 30 minutes

      meat for filling (shrimp, venison, chicken),
      cut into 1/4-inch squares
1   pkg. wonton skins
      vegetable oil
      eggs, beaten
      green onions, sliced

Fill wonton skins with meat of choice. Heat oil to 350 degrees and deep-fry meat pieces until slightly brown (about 3 minutes). Remove and drain on paper towels. Beat eggs. Separate wonton skins and flatten on plate. In center of each skin, place 1-2 pieces of meat and onion slices. Dip finger in beaten egg and rub connecting edges of wonton with egg. Fold opposite corner of wonton over, sealing edges together. Fold entire wonton and seal corners with egg.

Drop each wonton into hot oil and deep-fry until brown. Remove and drain on paper towels. Serve hot. For dipping, use sweet-and-sour sauce, hot mustard sauce, soy sauce, spicy garlic sauce or any favorite oriental dip.

Hunter's Safety ...

Alcohol, drugs and shooting do not mix. Drugs and alcohol may impair your judgment. Keen judgment is essential to safe shooting.

Stuffed Jalapenos

Serves: several
Prep Time: 30 minutes

18   whole jalapeno peppers
1   cup sharp cheddar cheese, grated
1   cup Monterey Jack cheese, grated
2   cups flour
2   eggs, beaten
2   cups fine bread crumbs
    oil

Use large, fresh jalapenos or large preserved peppers. Mix both cheeses together. Cut stem end off from each jalapeno and clean seeds and membranes from inside using small paring knife. Carefully stuff each pepper with cheese mixture without tearing outer skin. Roll each pepper in flour, dip in beaten eggs and roll in bread crumbs. Be sure that top opening of pepper is well covered by bread crumbs. Heat oil to 350 degrees in large saucepan. Deep-fry peppers until brown (2-3 minutes each), remove and drain on paper towels. Serve immediately.

Johnny B's Black Beans

Serves: 8
Prep Time: 30-45 minutes

1/2 lb. whiskey-fennel sausage*
1 T. whole cumin seed
5 tomatillos, chopped
2 large onions, chopped
2 whole jalapenos, chopped
1 carrot, peeled and shredded
black pepper to taste
white pepper to taste
1 red bell pepper, chopped
1 T. cider vinegar
2 cans black beans
2 T. chopped cilantro

Saute sausage in hot oil with cumin seed until brown. Add remaining ingredients, except cilantro. Cook slowly for 30 minutes. Stir in cilantro. Serve with rice and tortillas.

* See recipe for Whiskey Fennel Sausage (Big Game)

Susan Good
Novato, California

Baking Powder Drop Biscuits

Serves: 6 (yields 12 biscuits)
Prep Time: 20-30 minutes

 2   cups flour
 3   tsp. baking powder
 $1/2$ tsp. salt
 $1/2$ cup margarine
 $1^1/4$ cups milk

Preheat oven to 450 degrees. In large bowl, combine dry
ingredients. Cut margarine into flour mixture with fork
until it resembles coarse oatmeal. Add milk and stir mixture with fork to form ball. Drop batter by spoonfuls onto
greased cookie sheet. Bake for 8-12 minutes or until gold-
en brown.

Vivian Poyer
Rock Cave, West Virginia

Cool Sliced Tomatoes

Serves: several
Prep Time: 20 minutes

 2-3   large tomatoes (ripe)
 $1/2$ onion, chopped
 $1/2$ green pepper, chopped
 $1/4$ cup olive oil
 1   T. fresh lemon juice
 $1/2$ tsp. salt
 $1/2$ tsp. garlic, minced
 $1/2$ tsp. oregano
 $1/2$ tsp. fresh cilantro, minced

Slice tomatoes and arrange in deep dish. Combine other
ingredients and pour over tomatoes. Refrigerate for 1-2
hours before serving.

Tangy Grilled Potatoes

Serves: several
Prep Time: 30 minutes

6-10   red potatoes (small or medium)
       olive oil
       garlic powder
       Parmesan cheese (optional)
       sea salt

Boil potatoes until tender when pierced with fork.
Remove and let cool. Quarter potatoes and brush with
olive oil on all sides. Sprinkle garlic salt and Parmesan
cheese (if desired) over each piece, then dip in sea salt.
Arrange potato quarters on skewer or kabob stick. Grill
potatoes over coals until brown on outside.

Dill Cukes

Serves: several
Prep time: 30 minutes

2-3   large ripe cucumbers
 1   T. butter
      salt and pepper to taste
1/4   tsp. ground cumin
 3   T. fresh dill, chopped

Peel cucumbers and cut into 1-inch-thick slices; then cut
each slice in half. Steam cucumbers for $2^1/2$ minutes.
Remove from heat. In frying pan, melt butter. Add cucumbers, salt, pepper, cumin and dill. Stir-fry for about 1
minute. Serve immediately.

Potatoes Parmesan

Serves: several
Prep Time: 1 hour

5-6	large white potatoes
1/4	lb. butter
	sea salt to taste
1	cup Parmesan cheese, grated
1/2	T. fresh ground pepper, crushed

Peel potatoes and cut lengthwise into quarters, then halve each section. In cast-iron skillet, melt butter over medium heat and add potatoes, stirring until all wedges are covered with butter. Season potatoes with sea salt. Remove skillet and place in oven at 400 degrees for 20-25 minutes, stirring every 5-10 minutes. Meanwhile, mix Parmesan cheese with ground black pepper. Remove skillet from oven and sprinkle cheese over potatoes, mixing thoroughly. Continue to bake potatoes until brown (about 15 minutes). Remove and serve.

German Venison Salad

Serves: several
Prep Time: 30 minutes

3	cups cooked venison, chopped
1/4	cup Grey Poupon mustard
1/4	cup vinegar
1/4	cup brown sugar
2	cups mayonnaise
8	bacon slices, fried and chopped
6-8	green onions, chopped (with tops)
1/2	cup celery, finely chopped
2	red potatoes, cooked and diced

Mix mustard, vinegar and brown sugar together until smooth, then add mayonnaise; blend thoroughly. Fold in remaining ingredients. Chill and serve with crackers.

Venison Bean Soup

Serves: 3-4
Prep Time: 3 hours, 30 minutes

$1/2$	lb. venison, cut into $1/2$-inch cubes
1	cup dried navy beans
2-3	cups chicken stock
1	tsp. black pepper
$1/2$	tsp. cayenne pepper
$1/4$	tsp. thyme
$1/4$	tsp. sweet basil
1	large white potato, peeled and cubed
2	carrots, peeled and sliced into $1/4$-inch rounds
1	medium onion, chopped
	salt

Wash beans and remove unsatisfactory ones. Cover beans with water in large saucepan and bring to a boil for 2 minutes; remove from heat and let stand (covered) for 2 hours. Drain. Cover beans with fresh water and add 2-3 cups chicken stock; bring to a boil. Add seasonings and venison. Reduce heat and simmer for 1 hour, 30 minutes; stir occasionally. Add potato, carrots and onion. Simmer for 1 hour. Add salt to taste, if desired.

Hunter's Safety ...

Remember that firearms are precision instruments. If your gun is not working properly, do not hunt with it or take it shooting.

Delicious Tomato Pie

Serves: several
Prep Time: 1 hour

1	pie shell
3-4	tomatoes (ripe)
1	cup mozzarella cheese, shredded
1	T. fresh basil, chopped
3	T. butter, melted
	salt and pepper to taste
1/4	cup Parmesan cheese, ground

Prepare your favorite pie shell recipe or use frozen or pre-made shell. Slice tomatoes and drain on paper towels. Put mozzarella cheese on bottom pie crust and top with tomato slices. Spread basil evenly over tomatoes and drizzle butter over filling. Add salt and pepper to taste and top with Parmesan cheese. Preheat oven to 350 degrees and bake pie for 30 minutes. Remove from oven and allow to cool slightly before slicing.

Pheasant Salad

Serves: 3-4
Prep Time: 30-40 minutes

3	cups pheasant, cooked and cut into strips
	salt and pepper to taste
1/2	cup onion, chopped
1/4	cup celery, finely chopped
1/4	cup pecans or walnuts, chopped
1	cup mayonnaise
3/4	cup sour cream

Season meat with salt and pepper. Add remaining ingredients and mix well. Serve.

My Favorite Recipe

Recipe Name   ————————————————

Serves   ————————————————

Prep Time   ————————————————

Ingredients

————————————   ————————————————

————————————   ————————————————

————————————   ————————————————

————————————   ————————————————

————————————   ————————————————

————————————   ————————————————

————————————   ————————————————

————————————   ————————————————

Directions

————————————————————————

————————————————————————

————————————————————————

————————————————————————

————————————————————————

————————————————————————

————————————————————————

————————————————————————

————————————————————————

————————————————————————

————————————————————————

Index

240

Recipe Contributors

Contributing Members

Anderson, Richard
  Tunkhannock, PA, 190
Ball, Gary
  Warrens, WI, 52, 92
Barnes, Jack
  Dallas, TX, 64, 136
Bauman, Bill
  McKeesport, PA, 207
Beard, Robert
  Beaufort, SC, 54
Bellofatto, S.J.
  Columbus, GA, 112, 203, 206
Benson, Lawrence
  Oil City, PA, 161
Bernier, Norman
  Newington, CT, 162
Bingham, Patrick
  Tucson, AZ, 111, 113
Bitterman, Bruce
  Bismarck, ND, 70, 116, 124
Bollinger, Donald
  South Bend, IN, 198, 205
Bramer, Kurt
  Lakeville, MA, 40, 42
Bussard, Karen
  Felton, PA, 48, 62
Bussnick, Ray
  Emerson, NJ, 60, 175
Carl, Robert J.
  Blue Earth, MN, 205
Christman, Lyle
  Marysville, WA, 55
Coblentz, Willis
  Hartley, DE, 195
Coe, Steve
  Admire, KS, 50, 57
Coy, Dave
  Hoyt Lakes, MN, 135

Crump, Michael
  Peachtree City, GA, 45, 56
Daudier, Gerard
  Biddeford, ME, 191
Degel, Joel
  Puyallup, WA, 114, 116
Deperto, James
  Buffalo, NY, 39, 158, 177
DiGiampaolo, Joseph
  Raritan, NJ, 173
Dolick, Jeff
  San Antonio, TX, 75, 201
Dozier, Leigh
  Quartz Hill, CA, 137, 162
Duff, Ty
  Sparks, NV, 125, 126, 128
Eckles, Todd
  Hopedale, OH, 204
Farley, Kevin
  Beckley, WV, 83
Ferrell, C.R.
  Wilson, NC, 23, 44
Flategraff, Bradley
  Gallatin Gateway, MT, 117
Fogarty, Tim
  Westland, MI, 26
Frame, Phillip
  Sutton, WV, 170
Frederick, Bob
  New Britain, CT, 17
Garrett, Noel
  Gambrills, MD, 18, 20
Gassett, Ernest
  Wautoma, WI, 86
Good, Susan
  Novato, CA, 108, 110, 232
Hardee, Bill
  Norfolk, VA, 28, 171, 198

Great Gift Idea!

The NAHC Wild Game Cookbook!

Order extra copies of the 1994 Cookbook for
your friends and family. They make great gifts
—fun to read and practical as well!

You'll also like to have a second copy to keep
at the cabin or in with your camping gear.

Send your order in now and get yours at the
special Member's price of only $9.95 each.
(Non-members pay 14.95)

**Send me _____ copies of the 1994 Wild Game Cookbook,
I'm enclosing $9.95 each (non-members pay $14.95).
Include $2.83 per order for Postage and Handling.**

If paying by Check or Money Order, send this form in
an envelope with your payment to: NAHC Cookbook
P.O. Box 3402, Minneapolis, MN 55343
Charge customers may cut out this page, fold and mail.
(Don't forget to put on a stamp)

☐ Check here if you'd like to receive information about
ordering NAHC Wild Game Cookbooks from past years.

Payment Method:
Check or M.O.
——MasterCard
——Visa
——Discover

Card # —————————————
Exp. Date —————————————
Signature —————————————

Name ————————— Member # —————————
Address —————————————————————
City/State/Zip —————————————————

**North American Hunting Club
P. O. Box 3402
Minneapolis, MN 55343**

North American Hunting Club
P.O. Box 3402
Minneapolis, MN 55343

(tape or staple here)